COLLINS
# GEM
GUIDE

# FLAGS

# COLLINS GEM GUIDES

# FLAGS

## ▲ OF THE WORLD ▼

## COLLINS
### LONDON AND GLASGOW

Text: Edwin Moore and David Ross
Illustrations: Mike Saunders
Additional illustrations: Michelle McCluskie

First published 1986

ISBN 0 00 459503 3
Printed in Great Britain by Collins, Glasgow

# CONTENTS

# LIST OF ABBREVIATIONS
## USED IN THE TEXT

| | |
|---|---|
| AD | anno domini |
| admin. | administration, administered |
| agric. | agricultural, agriculture |
| auton. | autonomous |
| BC | before Christ |
| C | central |
| *c* | circa, about, approximately |
| cent. | century |
| dept. | department |
| E | east |
| esp. | especially |
| est. | estimated |
| estab. | established |
| *fl* | flourished |
| ft | feet |
| govt. | government |
| ha. | hectares |
| h.e.p. | hydro-electric power |
| incl. | includes, including |
| indust. | industry, industrial |
| isl. | island |
| km | kilometres |
| mi | miles |
| mt. | mountain |
| mts. | mountains |
| mfg. | manufacturing |
| N | north |

# INTRODUCTION

The history of flags stretches back 5,000 years and the uses to which they have been put are as different as their designs, shapes, sizes and colours.

Throughout the ages men have been stirred to acts of patriotism and bravery by following their family's or their country's flag into battle. Today flags are still used in war. But they are also used for the celebration of great events, and lesser ones. Bunting is strung up for coronations, jubilees and garden fetes. And on sadder occasions flags are flown at half-mast to honour the dead, and draped over the coffins of national heroes.

Vexillology is the scientific study of flags. The word comes from the Latin for standard.

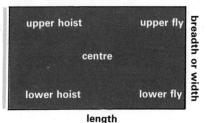

*The parts of a flag* have special names. The obverse is the side of a flag which you can see when the flagstaff is on the left and the reverse is the other side.

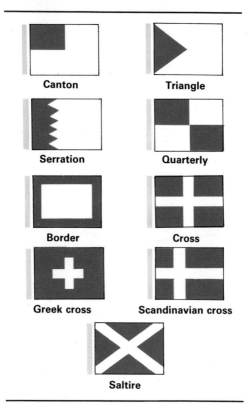

**Canton**

**Triangle**

**Serration**

**Quarterly**

**Border**

**Cross**

**Greek cross**

**Scandinavian cross**

**Saltire**

**Most modern flags** are rectangular but the pattern of colours (some derived from heraldry) varies. Many Christian countries' flags have a cross and four variations are shown opposite. However, in the past many different shapes of flags were used, some of which are shown below.

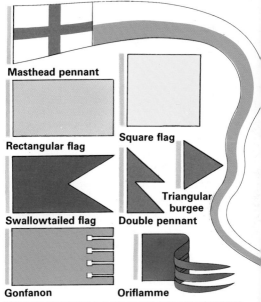

**Masthead pennant**

**Rectangular flag**

**Square flag**

**Swallowtailed flag**

**Double pennant**

**Triangular burgee**

**Gonfanon**

**Oriflamme**

Flags are mostly rectangular in shape today, but they were not always so. As flag design developed, many different shapes were used. In the Middle Ages flags helped the soldiers to tell their own units from those of the enemy in battle. Pennants of different shapes were tied to knights' lances, while long-tailed pennants and streamers were fixed to mastheads of ships for displays. Most of these shapes have now given way to the standard rectangular design, but the windsock which originated in Japan is still seen marking airfields.

Heraldry developed in Europe in medieval times, when knights and nobles painted designs on their shields and banners. These colourful symbols were essential, for, when a knight was clad from head to toe in armour, there was no other way of recognizing him.

The strict rules of heraldry have influenced the design of many of today's flags. Stripes, crosses and triangles abound. Coats of arms are still to be seen on many. But more modern symbols are used where they have a special significance, for example Canada's maple leaf, the crescent moon on the flags of Islamic nations and the five-pointed yellow star on the red flags of Communist countries.

*Heraldic shields* (opposite) are divided by partitions (per pale from top to bottom, per fess across, etc.). Charges are geometric shapes (chief, base, etc.). This heraldic influence can be traced in the design of many Western flags described later in this book.

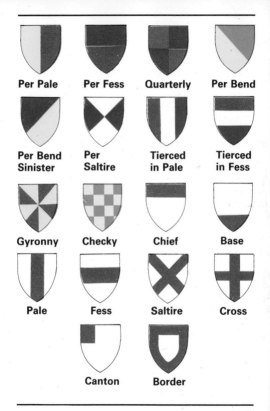

Per Pale    Per Fess    Quarterly    Per Bend

Per Bend Sinister    Per Saltire    Tierced in Pale    Tierced in Fess

Gyronny    Checky    Chief    Base

Pale    Fess    Saltire    Cross

Canton    Border

Religious symbols have appeared on flags from the earliest times. Christian armies carried the Cross into battle and the Virgin Mary was depicted on the banners of several Roman Catholic countries, while followers of Islam took the crescent moon symbol.

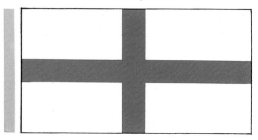

**Cross of St George**

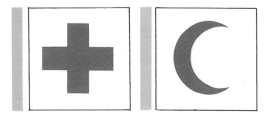

**Red Cross**          **Red Crescent**

**The Sikh flag**

Political parties within countries have their own flags, and sometimes these have been used as the basis of the design of a new national flag when a country has become independent. The flag of Angola, for example, is based on the black and red flag of the Popular Movement for the Liberation of Angola.

Many flags display features that link countries of similar background, culture and religion. The Pan-Arab colours of red, white, black and green are used by many Arab countries, while the Pan-African colours of red, yellow and green are flown by most black African states.

Some provinces or regions – such as the Cantons of Switzerland – have their own flags. Most cities use their national flags, but some have their own, often with symbols recording an event of historical importance.

Clubs, companies and organizations of people with similar interests have their own flags, too – many recognized throughout the world. The five circles of the Olympic flag represent the linking of the five continents in peaceful competition; and peace is also the message of the olive branches cradling the world in the flag of the United Nations.

**Olympic Flag**

**United Nations**

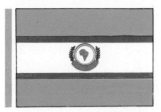

**Organization of African Unity**

**League of Arab States**

**Organization of American States**

**International Federation of Vexillological Associations**

**Flag of Mensa**

**World Scout Flag**

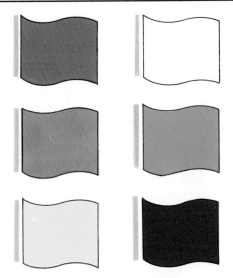

**The colours of flags** have developed special meanings. Red – danger, revolution, socialism, bloodshed of patriots; white – peace, surrender, truce; orange (or saffron) – courage, sacrifice; green – safety, proceed, Islam; yellow – sickness, caution; black – mourning, death, anarchy. Certain colours used together have particular meanings, for example the blue, white and red for the French tricolour is a symbol of liberty.

Flags have been used as a means of sending messages at sea since the eighteenth century. The first International Code was produced in 1857. It included 70,000 signals and employed 18 flags.

Since then the Code has been constantly updated and improved. As well as signifying a letter of the alphabet, each flag has a complete meaning of its own. Seamen still have to learn the correct method of hoisting the flags and how to interpret signals, even though electronic communication systems are now so sophisticated.

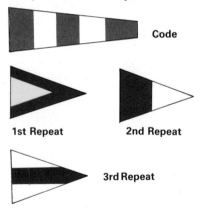

**Code**

**1st Repeat**

**2nd Repeat**

**3rd Repeat**

*Substitutes* allow the same signal flag – either alphabetical or numerical – to be repeated one or more times in the same group.

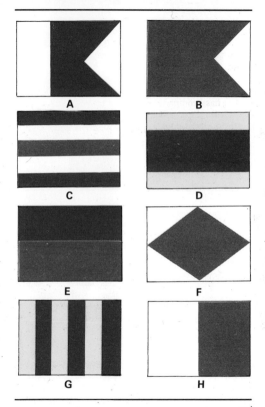

A

B

C

D

E

F

G

H

I

J

K

L

M

N

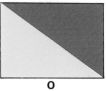

O

P

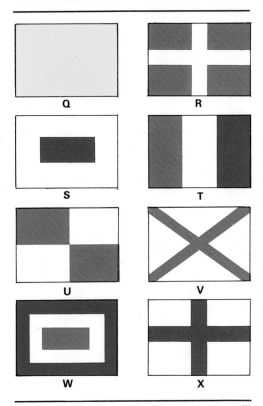

Q

R

S

T

U

V

W

X

Y

Z

1

2

3

4

5

6

7

8

9

10

# FLAGS
# OF THE
# WORLD

**AFGHANISTAN,** republic of SC Asia.
Area: 647,500 sq km (250,000 sq mi).
Population: 15,500,000 (est. 1979).
Capital: Kabul.
Language: Afghan.
Religion: Islam.
Dominated by Hindu Kush Mts; agric., stock rearing in river valleys and plains; dry continental climate.
Afghan kingdom created 1926; republic 1973; pro-Soviet regime estab. following Soviet invasion 1979; continuing guerilla war against govt.
**Flag**: after many changes from 1978, Afghanistan has readopted its traditional colours with the state arms in the canton.


**ALBANIA,** republic of SE Europe, on Adriatic.
Area: *c* 28,500 sq km (11,000 sq mi).
Population: 2,752,300 (1981).
Capital: Tirana.
Language: Albanian.
Religions: Islam, Eastern Orthodox.
Mountainous; lower marshy but fertile areas near coast; grows cereals, tobacco, olives.
Ruled by Turks 1468-1912; monarchy 1928-39; Communist republic under Hoxha estab. 1946; retains Stalinist policies; politically isolated.
**Flag**: dark red field bearing a two-headed black eagle emblem ('Albania' means 'land of the eagle'), with the Communist star (added in 1946) above.

**ALGERIA,** republic of N Africa.
Area: 2,388,000 sq km (922,000 sq mi).
Population: 20,200,000 (1983).
Capital: Algiers.
Languages: Arabic, French.
Religion: Islam.
Sahara in S; coastal plain, Atlas Mts. in N; cereals, dates, wine production; fishing; major oil and natural gas fields.
Former stronghold of Barbary pirates; occupied by French from 1830; revolution (1954-62) led to independence from France in 1962.
**Flag:** the traditional Islamic symbol and colours were adopted in 1962; the design is said to be based on a much earlier flag.


**ANDORRA,** principality of SW Europe in E Pyrenees.
Area: 495 sq km (191 sq mi).
Population: 41,600 (est. 1984)
Capital: Andorra la Vella.
Languages: Catalan, Spanish, French.
Religion: Roman Catholic.
Many high peaks, up to c 3050 m (10,000 ft); pasture (cattle, sheep), tobacco, fruit; tourism.
Traditionally said to have been granted independence by Charlemagne in 9th cent. after Moorish wars; under joint Franco-Spanish suzerainty since 1278.
**Flag:** adopted in 1866; the Andorran coat of arms is frequently imposed on the central (yellow) band.

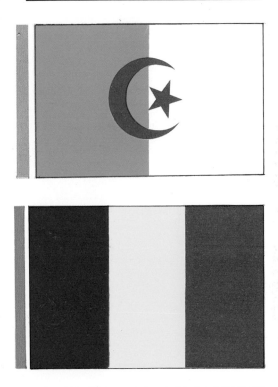

**ANGOLA,** republic of WC Africa.
Area: 1,246,600 sq km (481,300 sq mi).
Population: 7,100,000 (est. 1983).
Capital: Luanda.
Languages: Bantu, Portuguese.
Religions: native, Christian.
Narrow coastal strip, interior tableland; livestock, fishing; exports coffee, diamonds, oil.
Colonized 16th cent. by Portuguese; independent 1975; war between competing liberation groups ended (1976) in victory for the Marxist MPLA.
**Flag**: adopted in 1975, based on the Soviet Union-inspired MPLA flag; displays a yellow star, machete and half gear wheel imposed on two red and black bands.


**ANGUILLA,** island of E West Indies.
Area: 91 sq km (35 sq mi).
Population: *c* 7,000 (est. 1984).
Capital: The Valley.
Language: English.
Religion: Christian.
Flat coralline island, covered with low scrub; coral-sand beaches. Exports cotton, salt.
British colony since 1650; part of associate state of St Kitts-Nevis-Anguilla until 1980, when reverted to former status as a British dependency.
**Flag**: adopted in 1967; the white represents peace, the blue stripe hope and youth, the three dolphins strength.

**ANTIGUA and BARBUDA,** island of E West Indies.
Area: 280 sq km (108 sq mi).
Population: 78,000.
Capital: St John's.
Language: English.
Religion: Christian.
Dry climate; coral-sand beaches; sugar cane, cotton;
exports sugar, molasses, rum; tourism.
Discovered by Columbus 1493; colonized by British
1632; became associate state 1967; independent 1981;
British Commonwealth member.
**Flag**: adopted in 1967; the sun represents the new era,
the colours the people's dynamism (red), hope (blue),
the soil and African heritage (black), the sun, sea and
sand (gold, blue and white).

**ARGENTINA,** republic of S America.
Area: 2,776,889 sq km (1,072,157 sq mi).
Population: 27,862,771 (1980).
Capital: Buenos Aires.
Language: Spanish.
Religion: Roman Catholic.
Bounded by Andes on W and Atlantic on E; cotton,
beef, wheat, sheep rearing, oil.
Colonized by Spain in 16th cent.; independent 1810;
republic 1852; civilian govt. re-estab. 1983 after
successive military dictatorships.
**Flag**: blue and white were the colours flown *c* 1810 in the
independence struggle against Spain; a sun (not in
general use) representing emancipation was added in
1818.

**AUSTRALIA,** continent of SW Pacific Ocean.
Area: 7,690,000 sq km (2,970,000 sq mi).
Population: 15,451,900 (1983).
Capital: Canberra.
Language: English.
Religions: Anglican, Roman Catholic.
Narrow coastal lowlands; arid tableland in W; tropical to temperate climatic variation; rich in minerals and agriculture.
E coast claimed for Britain 1770; separate colonies federated in 1901 to form Federal Commonwealth; British Commonwealth member.
**Flag**: based on the Blue Ensign, adopted in 1901; the large star represents the Federal Commonwealth, the 5 small ones the Southern Cross.

**New South Wales:** St George's Cross with
a lion and four eight-pointed stars

**Queensland:** blue Maltese
Cross with royal crown

**South Australia:** white-backed piping shrike
(the Murray magpie) on a yellow field

 **Tasmania:** red lion on a white field

 **Victoria:** a crown over the Southern Cross

 **Western Australia:** black swan on a yellow field

 **Northern Territory:** Southern Cross and a desert rose on a brownish background

**AUSTRIA,** republic of C Europe.
Area: 83,851 sq km (32,375 sq mi).
Population: 7,551,300 (1983 est.).
Capital: Vienna.
Language: German.
Religion: Roman Catholic.
Mainly mountainous; fertile Danube plain in NE; cereals, cattle, pigs; industrial centres Vienna, Graz, Linz.
Ruled by Hapsburgs 1282-1918; centre of Holy Roman Empire; became Austrian empire in 1804; monarchy collapsed in 1918; part of Nazi Germany 1938-1945.
**Flag:** one of the oldest flags in continuous use, dating back to at least 1230; the colours may date from the Battle of Acre in 1191.

**BAHAMAS,** state of 700 isls. in N West Indies.
Area: 18,596 sq km (5382 sq mi).
Population: 135,437 (1980).
Capital: Nassau.
Language: English.
Religion: Christian.
Subsistence agriculture; exports some timber, fish, salt; important tourist industry; subject to hurricane damage.
Settled by British in 17th cent.; crown colony until independence 1973; British Commonwealth member.
**Flag:** adopted in 1973; the blue represents the sea, the yellow the sands, the black the strength and unity of the people.


**BAHRAIN,** isl. group of E Arabia in Persian Gulf.
Area: *c* 595 sq km (230 sq mi).
Population: 350,798 (1981).
Capital: Manama.
Language: Arabic.
Religion: Mainly Sunnite Islam.
Important oil reserves; dates grown; light industries.
Sheikdom under British protection until 1971; allied with United Arab Emirates.
**Flag:** in 1820 the British requested friendly states around the Persian Gulf to have white on their flags; separated from the traditional Muslim red by a serrated line. See also Qatar.

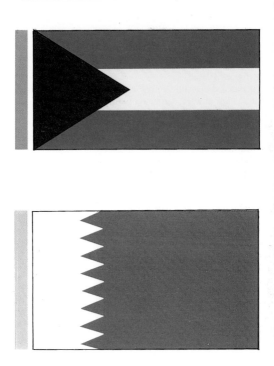

**BANGLADESH,** republic of SC Asia.
Area: *c* 143,000 sq km (55,200 sq mi).
Population: 89,940,000 (1981).
Capital: Dacca.
Language: Bengali.
Religion: Islam.
Includes deltas of Ganges and Brahmaputra rivers; densely populated; agric. economy based on rice, tea, jute; subject to flooding and cyclones.
Part of British India until 1947; part of Pakistan as East Pakistan until secession and civil war 1971; British Commonwealth member.
**Flag**: adopted in 1971; the green field represents fertility, the red disc the struggle for freedom.


**BARBADOS,** isl. state of E West Indies.
Area: 430 sq km (166 sq mi).
Population: 248,983 (1980).
Capital: Bridgetown.
Language: English.
Religion: Christian.
Fertile soil; sugar cane growing; molasses, rum; winter tourist resort; subject to hurricanes.
Claimed by Britain 1605; independent 1966; British Commonwealth member.
**Flag**: adopted in 1966; the shaft of the trident is broken to represent independence and the nation's break with the past; the blue represents the sea and sky, gold the sand of the beaches.

**BELGIUM,** kingdom of NW Europe.

Area: 30,510 sq km (11,780 sq mi).

Population: 9,863,374 (1981).

Capital: Brussels.

Languages: Flemish (N), Walloon French (S).

Religion: Roman Catholic.

Sandy area in N (Flanders), fertile plain in C, forested plateau in SE (Ardennes); cereals, flax, livestock, extensive trade along North Sea coast; coal mining and heavy industry.

Ruled by Burgundy, Hapsburgs, Spain, France, Netherlands; independent monarchy from 1830.

**Flag:** the present almost square flag was adopted in 1830; the colours derive from the arms of the Province of Brabant.


**BELIZE,** state on E coast of Central America.

Area: 22,965 sq km (8867 sq mi).

Population: 148,300 (1981).

Capital: Belmopan.

Language: English.

Religion: Christian.

Densely forested; Maya Mts. in interior; tropical climate; grows sugar cane, citrus fruit; timber exports; fish packing; occasional hurricanes.

Formerly known as British Honduras; independent 1981; unresolved territ. dispute with Guatemala; British Commonwealth member.

**Flag:** adopted in 1968; the coat of arms displays two men, logging industry tools, and the motto 'I flourish in the shade'.

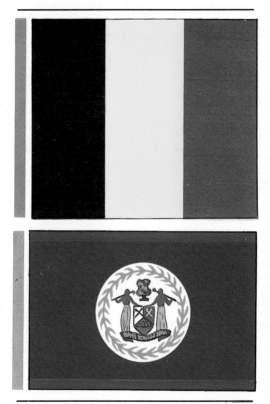

**BENIN,** republic of W Africa.
Area: 112,700 sq km (43,500 sq mi).
Population: 3,338,240 (1979).
Capital: Porto Novo.
Language: French.
Religions: native, Roman Catholic.
Subsistence agric.; exports coffee, cotton, palm oil; small mineral deposits.
Native kingdom 17th-19th cent., promoted slave trade; colonized 1892-3 by French; independent 1960; became a People's Republic in 1975; formerly known as Dahomey.
**Flag:** adopted in 1975; the green represents the agricultural economy, the red star national unity and revolution.

**BERMUDA,** coral isl. group of *c* 300 isls. in NC Atlantic.
Area: 52 sq km (20 sq mi).
Population: 57,237 (1980).
Capital: Hamilton.
Language: English.
Religion: Christian.
Industry based on year-round US tourism.
Discovered by Spanish 1515; settled by British 1609; British crown colony.
**Flag:** the Red Ensign with the coat of arms dates from 1915; a red lion holds the wreck of the *Sea Venture*, on which the first settlers arrived in 1609.

**BHUTAN,** kingdom of SC Asia.
Area: *c* 47,000 sq km (18,000 sq mi).
Population: 1,300,000 (est. 1981).
Capital: Thimbu.
Language: Tibetan variant.
Religion: Mahayana Buddhism.
Infertile and mountainous N region (Himalayas), C zone of upland valleys, S forested foothills; agric. and animal husbandry; mineral resources.
Parts of S annexed by British in 19th cent.; Indian protect. from 1949.
**Flag:** adopted on UN entry, the saffron represents royal power, the orange-red Buddhist spiritual power; the dragon is Bhutan's national symbol.


**BOLIVIA,** republic of C South America.
Area: 1,098,580 sq km (424,162 sq mi).
Population: 6,000,000 (est. 1984).
Capitals: Sucre, La Paz (administrative).
Languages: Spanish, Quechua, Aymara, Guarani.
Religion: Roman Catholic.
Andes and tableland in W, tropical rain forests in NE, Chaco plain in SE; important tin, silver, copper mines; agric. crops include rice and wheat.
Native Indians (Inca ruled) overrun by Spanish in 16th cent.; independent 1824; wars with neighbouring states reduced territory.
**Flag:** the colours date from *c* 1825; the red represents the army's valour, the yellow mineral resources, the green agricultural wealth.

22

**BOTSWANA,** republic of S Africa.
Area: 600,000 sq km (231,000 sq mi).
Population: 937,000 (1981).
Capital: Gaborone.
Languages: Tswana, English.
Religions: native, Christian.
Mainly dry plateau, Okavango Swamp in N, Kalahari Desert in S; nomadic pastoralism, exports cattle, hides; main crops maize, millet.
Created Bechuanaland Protect. 1885; independent 1966; British Commonwealth member.
**Flag**: adopted in 1966; the black-and-white zebra stripe represents the racial harmony of the people, the blue bands rain and water (the national motto is 'Let there be rain').

**BRAZIL,** republic of E South America.
Area: 8,511,965 sq km (3,286,470 sq mi).
Population: 119,098,922 (1980).
Capital: Brasilia.
Language: Portuguese.
Religion: Roman Catholic.
Extensive Atlantic coastline; mainly agric. esp. coffee, cotton, sugar cane; undeveloped interior (tropical rainforest) and mineral resources.
Portuguese settlement from 16th cent.; independent 1882; republic 1889.
**Flag**: based on the flag of Portugal; the central sphere bears the motto 'Order and Progress'; the 23 stars represent the states and Federal District.

**BRUNEI,** sultanate of N Borneo.
Area: *c* 5760 sq km (2200 sq mi).
Population: *c* 200,000 (1982).
Capital: Bandar Seri Begawan.
Languages: Malay, English.
Religion: Islam.
Rubber and fruit growing; rich oil and gas deposits.
Under British protection since 1888; internally self-governing from 1971; independent 1984; British Commonwealth member.
**Flag**: a white and a black stripe representing British protection were added to the Sultan's plain yellow flag in 1906; in 1959 the state arms were added.


**BULGARIA,** republic of SE Europe, on Black Sea.
Area: 110,899 sq km (42,818 sq mi).
Population: 8,929,000 (1982).
Capital: Sofia.
Languages: Bulgarian, Turkish.
Religions: Eastern Orthodox, Islam.
Mountainous; lowland in N and SE; cereals, tobacco, wine; coal, oil; indust. development.
Invaded 7th cent. by Bulgars; Turkish rule 1395-1878 ended by Russia; independent monarchy from 1908; Communist govt. estab. in 1946.
**Flag**: the Slav colours of white, green and red were used from 1878; the national emblem with lion (symbol of Bulgaria since 14th cent.) was added in 1947.

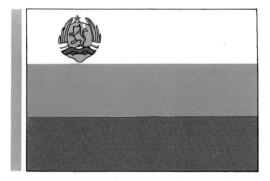

**BURKINA,** republic of W Africa.
Area: 274,300 sq km (105,900 sq mi).
Population: 6,600,000 (est. 1979).
Capital: Ouagadougou.
Language: French.
Religions: native, Islam, Roman Catholic.
Landlocked plateau, mainly savannah and semidesert; maize, millet, groundnuts, livestock.
French colony from 1919; independent as Upper Volta 1960; coups in 1980, 1982, 1983; changed its name to Burkina 1984.
**Flag:** a new flag using the Pan-African colours to represent African unity was adopted in 1984.

**BURMA,** republic of SE Asia.
Area: *c* 678,000 (262,000 sq mi).
Population: 35,313,905 (1983).
Capital: Rangoon.
Language: Burmese.
Religion: Buddhism.
Mountainous; agric. concentrated around Irrawaddy valley; rice growing; exports teak, petroleum.
Annexed by Britain in 19th cent.; became prov. of India 1885-1937; independent republic 1948; socialist republic from 1962 following coup.
**Flag:** a socialist symbol was added to the flag in 1974; a ring of 14 stars representing the 14 states surrounds a gearwheel and a rice plant, showing the union of industry and agriculture.

**BURUNDI,** republic of EC Africa.
Area: 27,800 sq km (10,750 sq mi).
Population: 4,480,000 (est. 1984).
Capital: Bujumbura.
Languages: Bantu, French.
Religions: native, Christian.
Mainly high broken plateau; Lake Tanganyika in SW; cattle rearing, tin mining; exports coffee.
Part of German East Africa from 1899; Belgian colony after WWI; UN Trust Territ. from 1946; independence in 1962; republic in 1966.
**Flag:** adopted in 1966; the stars represent the nation's motto 'Unity, Work, Progress'; the colours represent peace (white), hope (green), and the struggle for independence (red).

**CAMEROON,** republic of WC Africa.
Area: 474,000 sq km (183,000 sq mi).
Population: 8,320,000 (est. 1980).
Capital: Yaoundé.
Languages: French, English.
Religions: Christian, Islam.
Savannah in N; tropical forest in W; produces cocoa, coffee, bananas, groundnuts, bauxite.
Formerly German; taken by Allies in WWI; divided (1919) into French and British Cameroons; UN Trust Territs. from 1946; United Republic in 1972.
**Flag:** adopted in 1960, based on the tricolour of France; two stars representing the British Cameroons were added in 1961, and replaced by a single star to represent unity in 1972.

**CANADA,** federal dominion of N North America.
Area: 9,976,128 sq km (3,851,787 sq mi).
Population: 24,343,181 (1981).
Capital: Ottawa.
Languages: English, French.
Religions: Protestant, Roman Catholic.
Extends from Pacific to Atlantic, from Arctic to the
Great Lakes; extreme climate; timber, agric., wheat;
fisheries, mining, industry.
Settled by French in 17th cent.; British dominance from
1759; independent 1867; enlarged by W expansion;
British Commonwealth member.

**Flag:** the Red Ensign was used from 1892, but was
unpopular with the French community; the present
design with maple leaf emblem was adopted in 1965.

**Alberta**

**British Columbia**

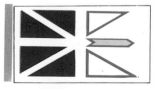

**Newfoundland**

**Nova Scotia**

**Manitoba**

**New Brunswick**

**Northwest Territories**

**Prince Edward Island**

**Ontario**

**Quebec**

**Saskatchewan**

**Yukon**

**CAPE VERDE ISLANDS,** republic of EC Atlantic.
Area: 4040 sq km (1560 sq mi).
Population; 296,093 (1980).
Capital: Praia.
Language: Portuguese.
Religion: Roman Catholic.
Comprises two groups of isls. of volcanic origin; stock raising, fishing; exports coffee, fruit.
Colonized 15th cent. by Portuguese; independent 1975; planned federation with Guinea-Bissau cancelled following 1980 coup in latter.
**Flag:** the Pan-African colours were adopted in 1975; the emblem's five-pointed black star is above a garland of maize sheaves, two corn cobs and a clamshell.

**CAYMAN ISLANDS,** coral isl. group of West Indies.
Area: 260 sq km (100 sq mi).
Population. 18,750 (1983).
Capital: Georgetown.
Language: English.
Religion: Christian.
Turtles and turtle products; shark skin exports.
Administered by Jamaica until 1962; British crown colony.
**Flag**: the coat of arms on the blue ensign was granted in 1958, and displays a turtle, a pineapple, three stars to represent the main islands, with the motto 'He hath founded it upon the seas.'


**CENTRAL AFRICAN REPUBLIC,** state of C Africa.
Area: 623,000 sq km (241,000 sq mi).
Population: 2,379,000 (1981).
Capital: Bangui.
Languages: Sangho, French.
Religions: native, Christian.
Largely savannah-covered plateau, tropical forest in S; cotton, coffee growing; diamond, uranium mining.
Formerly part of French Equatorial Africa; independent 1960; became Central African Empire under Bokhassa 1976; reverted to republic in 1979.
**Flag**: adopted in 1960; the Pan-African and French colours represent the friendship between the two nations.

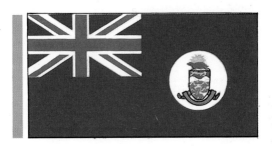

**CHAD,** republic of NC Africa.
Area: 1,284,000 sq km (495,000 sq mi).
Population: 4,000,000 (est. 1984).
Capital: Ndjamena.
Language: French.
Religions: native, Christian, Islam.
Savannah in S; desert and mts. in N; Lake Chad in S; cotton, peanut-growing in S; nomadic pastoralism in N. Formerly part of French Equatorial Africa; independence in 1960; coups in 1975 and 1979.
**Flag**: adopted in 1959; the colours are a compromise between the French and Pan-African flags; blue represents the sky, yellow the sun and desert, red the national sacrifice.


**CHILE,** republic of W South America.
Area: 756,945 sq km (292,256 sq mi).
Population: 11,000,000 (est. 1979).
Capital: Santiago.
Language: Spanish.
Religion: Roman Catholic.
Comprises narrow coastal strip W of Andes extending S to Tierra del Fuego; important mineral resources; sheep and cattle rearing.
Conquered by Spanish in 16th cent.; independent 1818; Marxist government elected in 1970; right-wing military coup in 1973.
**Flag**: inspired by the US Stars and Stripes and adopted in 1817; white represents the Andean snow, blue the sky, red the blood of the patriots.

**CHINA, People's Republic of,** state of E Asia.
Area: *c* 9,561,000 sq km (3,691,500 sq mi).
Population: 1,008,175,288 (1982).
Capital: Peking.
Language: Mandarin and other forms of Chinese.
Religions: Confucianism, Buddhism, Shintoism.
Mountainous in N and W; fertile valleys, plains in E; climate extreme in N, subtropical in S; rice, wheat growing; textile mfg.; great mineral wealth.
Ruled by imperial dynasties until 1912; republic 1911; Communist govt. estab.1949.
**Flag:** adopted in 1949; red is the traditional colour of both Communism and China; the large star represents the party's programme, the small ones the four social classes it unites.

**COLOMBIA,** republic of NW South America.
Area: 1,138,900 sq km (439,700 sq mi).
Population: 28,100,000 (est. 1981).
Capital: Bogota.
Language: Spanish.
Religion: Roman Catholic.
Andes in W; tropical forests, grasslands in E; coffee and banana crops; mineral resources.
Spanish colony from 16th cent.; independent 1819; known as New Granada until 1863; Panama seceded in 1903; civil war 1949-53.
**Flag:** adopted in 1861; yellow represents the nation, separated by the sea (blue) from Spain, whose tyranny the people resisted with their blood (red). See also Ecuador and Venezuela.

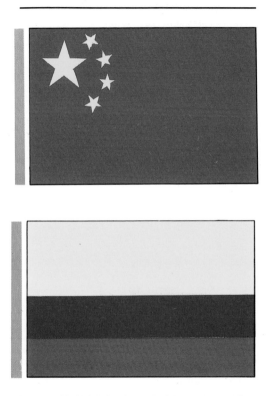

**COMORO ISLANDS,** republic in Indian Ocean.
Area: 2170 sq km (838 sq mi).
Population: 385,000 (est. 1979).
Capital: Moroni.
Language: French.
Religions: Islam, Christian.
Volcanic isls.; produces vanilla, copra, cocoa, coffee, cloves, timber.
Formerly French overseas territ.; the island of Mayotte voted to remain a French dependency on the formation of the republic in 1975.
**Flag**: adopted in 1975; the crescent represents the islanders' Islamic faith, the stars the four islands (including the French dependency of Mayotte).

**CONGO (BRAZZAVILLE),** republic of WC Africa.
Area: 342,000 sq km (132,000 sq mi).
Population: *c* 2,100,000 (est. 1984).
Capital: Brazzaville.
Languages: Bantu, French.
Religions: native, Christian.
Mainly tropical forest; exports hardwoods, sugar, tobacco, coffee; cassava, yam crops; lead mining.
Explored 15th cent. by Portuguese; part of French Equatorial Africa from 1910; independent 1960; People's Republic 1970.
**Flag**: a design based on the USSR flag and using the Pan-African colours was adopted in 1970; the crossed hammer and hoe represents the union between industry and agriculture.

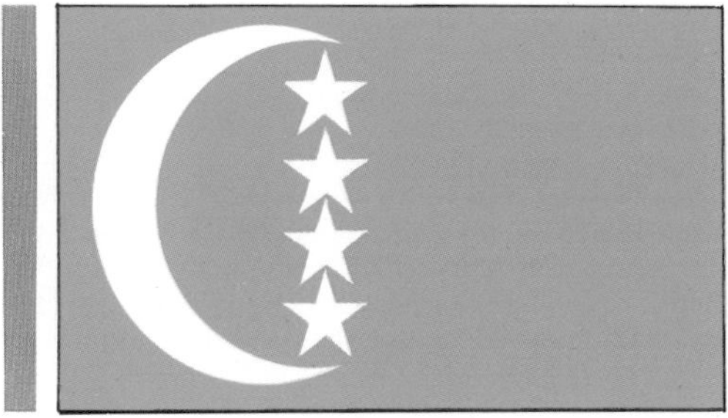

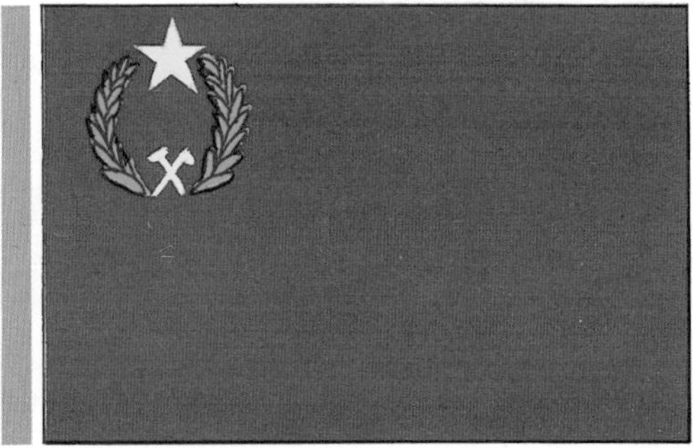

**COOK ISLANDS,** isl. group of SC Pacific Ocean.
Area: 240 sq km (93 sq mi).
Population: 17,400 (est. 1983).
Capital: main island Rarotonga.
Language: English.
Religion: Christian.
Volcanic and coral isls.; exports fruit, copra, pearl shell.
Administered by New Zealand from 1901; incorporated
within dominion 1907; self-governing from 1965.
**Flag:** a design based on the Blue Ensign was adopted in
1973; the fifteen stars represent each island in the group.

**COSTA RICA:** republic of Central America.
Area: 50,700 sq km (19,575 sq mi).
Population: 2,276,676 (est. 1981).
Capital: San José.
Language: Spanish.
Religion: Roman Catholic.
Dormant volcanic mts. with jungle in N; plains on
coasts; exports coffee, bananas, timber.
Part of Guatemala under Spanish rule until 1821; part of
Central American Federation 1823-38; army abolished
1948.
**Flag:** adopted in 1848; retains the blue/white/blue
sequence of the Federation flag, with an additional red
stripe.

**CUBA,** isl. republic in West Indies.
Area: 114,525 sq km (44,218 sq mi).
Population: 9,939,800 (est. 1983).
Capital: Havana.
Language: Spanish.
Religion: Roman Catholic.
Mainly lowland; mountainous interior and SE; exports sugar, tobacco, fruit, timber.
Settled by Spanish in 16th cent.; independent 1902 after Spanish-American War; Communist govt. estab. after 1958 revolt against Batista regime.
**Flag**: officially adopted in 1902, the 'Lone Star' banner is based on the US flag and dates from 1849; the red triangle represents freedom from Spain.


**CYPRUS,** isl. republic in E Mediterranean.
Area: 9270 sq km (3572 sq mi).
Population: 618,300 (est. 1978).
Capital: Nicosia.
Languages: Greek, Turkish.
Religions: Eastern Orthodox, Islam.
Irrigated plain between two mountain ranges; pastoral economy; grain, wine, olives grown.
Ruled by Assyria, Persia, Rome, Turkey, Britain; independent 1960; Greek/Turkish conflict 1950-64; Turkish invasion and de facto partition in 1974; British Commonwealth member.
**Flag**: adopted in 1960; the two olive branches represent Greek/Turkish unity; the separate communities now fly their own national flags.

**CZECHOSLOVAKIA,** republic of EC Europe.
Area: 127,842 sq km (49,360 sq mi).
Population: 15,280,148 (1980).
Capital: Prague.
Languages: Czech, Slovak.
Religion: Roman Catholic.
Bohemian plateau in W, Moravian lowland in C, Slovakian highlands, Carpathians in E; grows cereals, sugar beet; timber, coal, iron industries.
Formed (1918) from parts of Austria-Hungary; occupied by Germany 1938-45; coup estab. Communist govt. in 1948; Soviet invasion in 1968.
**Flag**: adopted in 1920; combines the Bohemian red and white with the Moravian and Slovakian blue, the colours of 19th-cent. Pan-Slavic liberation.

**DENMARK,** kingdom of NC Europe.
Area: 43,022 (16,611 sq mi).
Population: 5,116,464 (1982).
Capital: Copenhagen.
Language: Danish.
Religion: Lutheranism.
Comprises Jutland penin. and several Baltic isls; dairy produce and livestock; fishing.
United with Sweden 1397-1523, with Norway 1397-1814; lost Norway and Schleswig-Holstein in 19th-cent. wars; occupied by Germany 1940-5.
**Flag**: possibly the oldest national flag in continuous use; the white cross against a red field represents King Waldemar II's vision before the Battle of Lyndanisse in 1219.

**DJIBOUTI,** state of NE Africa.
Area: 22,000 sq km (8,500 sq mi).
Population: 300,000 (est. 1984).
Capital: Djibouti.
Language: French.
Religion: Islam.
Port, railway to Addis Ababa; transit trade, exports cattle, hides, salt.
Formerly known as French Somaliland and then the French Territory of the Afars and the Issas; independent 1977.
**Flag:** adopted by the independence movement in 1972; the blue represents the Issas and green the Afars; the white is for peace and the star for unity.


**DOMINICA,** isl. republic of SE West Indies.
Area: 750 sq km (290 sq mi).
Population: 74,069 (1981).
Capital: Roseau.
Language: English.
Religion: Christian.
Mainly mountainous with much volcanic activity; fruit growing; rum, copra exports.
Former Carib stronghold; successive French, British occupation, then British colony; republic in 1978; British Commonwealth member.
**Flag:** adopted in 1978; the parrot is the national bird, the 'sisserou', and was retained from the coat of arms on the old Blue Ensign; the 10 stars represent the 10 island parishes.

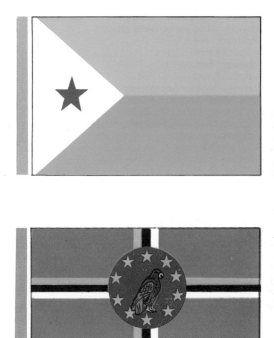

**DOMINICAN REPUBLIC,** republic of West Indies.
Area: 48,734 sq km (18,816 sq mi).
Population: 5,647,977 (1981).
Capital: Santo Domingo.
Language: Spanish.
Religion: Roman Catholic.
Mountainous interior; agric. land in E; sugar, coffee,
cocoa, tobacco; bauxite, salt mining.
Discovered by Columbus in 1492; settled by Spanish;
independent 1844; US military rule 1916-24; Trujillo
dictatorship 1930-61.
**Flag**: adopted in 1844; the white cross represents the
liberation movement over the former blue and red
'French' flag of Haiti, of which the Republic was once a
part.

**ECUADOR,** republic of NW South America.
Area: 283,561 sq km (109,483 sq mi).
Population: *c* 8,000,000 (est. 1981).
Capital: Quito.
Language: Spanish.
Religion: Roman Catholic.
Pacific coast plain rises to Andes; exports bananas,
coffee; subsistence agric. in mountains.
Spanish colony from 16th cent.; part of Peru until
liberated 1822; independent 1830 at dissolution of
Greater Colombia.
**Flag**: linked with Colombia and Venezuela until 1830,
Ecuador shares with them the flag under which Simon
Bolivar's armies marched. See also Colombia and
Venezuela.

**EGYPT,** republic of NE Africa.
Area: 1,001,000 sq km (386,500 sq mi).
Population: 47,000,000 (est. 1983).
Capital: Cairo.
Language: Arabic.
Religion: Islam.
Largely desert; fertile Nile valley produces rice, cotton, cereals; petroleum, phosphates.
Ancient Egypt ruled by 30 dynasties; subsequent rulers incl. Rome, Arabs, Turks, French, and British; monarchy 1923; republic 1953.
**Flag**: the Pan-Arab colours of red, black and white were adopted in 1972 to symbolize the unity of Egypt with Libya and Syria; under the hawk is the motto 'Federation of Arab Republics'.

**EL SALVADOR,** republic of Central America.
Area: 21,393 sq km (8260 sq mi).
Population: 4,939,400 (est. 1981).
Capital: San Salvador.
Language: Spanish.
Religion: Roman Catholic.
Pacific coastline rises to fertile plain; volcanic mts.; cotton, coffee, balsam; cattle rearing.
Under Spanish rule 1524-1821; member of Central American Federation until independence (1838); civil strife unresolved by 1982 elections.
**Flag**: the traditional Central American colours were adopted in 1912; two variations are allowed, one bears the motto 'God, Union, Liberty', the other the coat of arms.

**EQUATORIAL GUINEA,** republic of WC Africa.
Area: 28,000 sq km (10,800 sq mi).
Population: 150,000 (est. 1980).
Capital: Rey Malabo.
Languages: Bantu, Spanish.
Religions: native, Roman Catholic.
Comprises Bioco, Pagalu, Corisco isls. and Riu Muni mainland; hot, wet climate; exports coffee, cocoa, hardwoods.
Colony as Spanish Guinea from 18th cent.; independence in 1968; military coup in 1979; parliamentary elections in 1983.
**Flag**: adopted in 1968; green represents the nation's natural resources, blue is for the sea, white is for peace, and red for independence.

**ETHIOPIA,** republic of NE Africa.
Area: 1,222,000 sq km (472,000 sq mi).
Population: 31,000,000 (est. 1981).
Capital: Addis Ababa.
Language: Amharic.
Religions: Coptic Christianity, Islam.
High plateau bisected from NE-SW by Great Rift Valley; subsistence agric.; exports coffee, hides.
Aksumite empire 1st-7th cent. declined after Moslem incursions; reunited 19th cent., defeated Italian invasion 1896; occupied by Italy 1936-41; Emperor deposed by military coup in 1974; famine and civil war with Eritrean rebels (1985).
**Flag**: first flown as three separate pennants; the present order has been used since 1941.

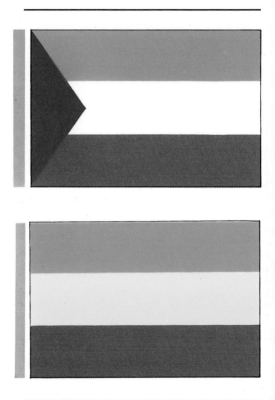

**FAEROES,** isl. group of Denmark, in N Atlantic between Iceland and the Shetlands.
Area: 1399 sq km (540 sq mi).
Population: 41,211 (1976).
Capital: Thorshavn.
Language: Danish.
Religion: Lutheranism.
Rugged and treeless; sheep rearing; fishing.
Colonized by Norse settlers in 9th cent.; passed from Norway to Denmark in 1380; auton. legislature from 1948.
**Flag**: adopted in 1948, the cross is, like other Scandinavian flags, slightly off-centre; combines local arms with those of Denmark.

**FALKLAND ISLANDS,** crown colony of UK, in S Atlantic Ocean.
Area: 12,100 sq km (4700 sq mi).
Population: 1,813 (1980).
Capital: Stanley.
Language: English.
Religion: Christian.
Sheep rearing.
Discovered by British 1592; French settlement in 1764, then sold to Spain, who recognized British claim in 1771; British resettlement from 1833; Argentina's claim to sovereignty led to invasion and war in 1982.
**Flag**: flies the Blue Ensign; the sheep on the badge represents the islands' wealth, and the ship is the *Desire*, which discovered the islands.

**FIJI ISLANDS,** country of SW Pacific Ocean.
Area: 18,350 sq km (7080 sq mi).
Population: 671,712 (1983).
Capital: Suva.
Languages: English, Fijian.
Religions: Christian, Hindu.
Produces sugar cane, rice, fruit, gold; tourism.
British colony from 1874; large immigration of indentured labourers from India 1879-1919; independent 1970; British Commonwealth member.
**Flag**: a design based on the Blue Ensign was adopted in 1970; the coat of arms displays the British lion (holding a cocoa pod), sugar cane, a coconut palm, a bunch of bananas and a dove of peace.


**FINLAND,** republic of NE Europe.
Area: 337,010 sq km (130,120 sq mi).
Population: 4,844,000 (1982).
Capital: Helsinki.
Languages: Finnish, Swedish.
Religion: Lutheranism.
Tundra in N, mainly within Arctic Circle; lakes, forests in S; forestry, some agric.; pulp and paper indust.
Conquered by Erik IX of Sweden in 12th cent.; ceded to Russia 1809; independent 1917; republic estab. 1919; lost territ. to USSR after war of 1939-40.
**Flag**: adopted in 1917; the blue and white represents the nation's lakes and snowfields.

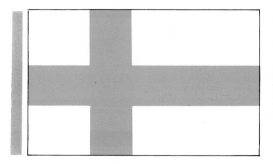

**FRANCE,** republic of W Europe.
Area: *c* 547,000 sq km (211,000 sq mi).
Population: 54,334,871 (1982).
Capital: Paris.
Language: French.
Religion: Roman Catholic.
Incl. Alps and Pyrenees; fertile lowlands; cereals, livestock, vineyards; indust.; tourism.
Roman prov. until 5th cent.; Frankish kingdom estab. 9th cent.; Revolution (1789) and Napoleonic Wars; monarchic restorations; Fifth Republic 1958.
**Flag**: adopted in 1794; based on an earlier flag using red and blue to represent Paris, and white for the monarchy, the more austere 1794 design is meant to symbolize republican principles.

**GABON,** republic of WC Africa.
Area: 268,000 sq km (103,500 sq mi).
Population: 1,200,000 (est. 1982).
Capital: Libreville.
Languages: Bantu, French.
Religions: native, Roman Catholic.
Coastal plain, interior plateau; largely tropical rain-forest; exports petroleum, manganese, hardwoods.
Reached by Portuguese 1485; slave trade 17th-19th cent.; part of French Congo from 1886, of French Equatorial Africa from 1908; independent 1960.
**Flag**: adopted in 1960; green represents the forests and the lumber industry, blue the sea, and yellow the sun.

**GAMBIA,** republic of W Africa.

Area: 10,360 sq km (4,000 sq mi).

Population: *c* 700,000 (1983).

Capital: Banjul.

Language: English.

Religions: native, Islam.

Smallest African country, surrounded by Senegal; exports groundnuts, hides.

Discovered in 15th cent. by Portuguese; British colony from 1843; independent 1965; formed Senegambia Confederation with Senegal 1982; British Commonwealth member.

**Flag:** adopted in 1965; the design represents the Gambia river (blue) flowing through the green land with the sun overhead.

**GERMANY, EAST,** republic of NC Europe.

Area: *c* 108,000 sq km (42,000 sq mi).

Population: 16,740,000 (1980).

Capital: East Berlin.

Language: German.

Religions: Protestant, Roman Catholic.

Low, sandy plain in N; mountains, forest in C; industs. centred in Saxony.

Part of Holy Roman Empire 962-1806, and of united Germany 1871-1945; lost much territ. in WWII; partition from West Germany in 1949 and estab. of Communist state.

**Flag:** the colours are expressive of federal unity, and date from the early 19th cent.; the state emblem was added in 1959.

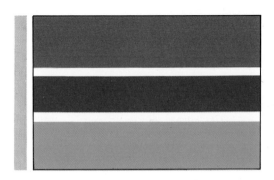

**GERMANY, WEST,** republic of NC Europe.
Area: *c* 249,000 sq km (96,000 sq mi).
Population: 61,333,000 (1983).
Capital: Bonn.
Language: German.
Religions: Protestant, Roman Catholic.
Low, sandy plain in N; mountains, forest in C; Rhine
valley in W; Alps in S; industs. centred in Ruhr.
Part of Holy Roman Empire 962-1806, and of united
Germany 1871-1945; lost much territ. in WWII;
partition from East Germany in 1949.
**Flag:** adopted in 1949; the colours are associated with
federal unity and date from the early 19th cent.

**GHANA,** republic of W Africa, on Gulf of Guinea.
Area: 238,500 sq km (92,100 sq mi).
Population: *c* 14,000,000 (est. 1984).
Capital: Accra.
Language: English.
Religions: native, Christian.
Largely forest, with savannah in N; main river Volta;
produces cocoa, hardwoods, gold, diamonds.
Former centre of slave trade; British colony estab. 1874;
independent 1957; republic from 1960; British Com-
monwealth member.
**Flag:** adopted in 1957; the Pan-African colours here
represent the blood of the freedom fighters (red),
mineral wealth (gold) and the rich forest (green); the star
symbolizes African freedom.

**GIBRALTAR,** British colony of S Iberian penin., between Atlantic and Mediterranean.

Area: 6.5 sq km (2.5 sq mi).

Population: 28,719 (1981).

Language: English.

Religion: Christian.

Rises to 425 m (1400 ft); free port, heavily fortified naval base; tourist resort.

One of the ancient 'Pillars of Hercules'; Moorish stronghold from 8th cent.; held by Spain 1462-1704; UK dependency (disputed by Spain) from 1713.

**Flag:** officially flies the Union Jack, but the city flag representing the fortified gateway to the Mediterranean is more often seen.


**GREECE,** republic of SE Europe.

Area: 132,000 sq km (50,900 sq mi).

Population: 9,740,417 (1981).

Capital: Athens.

Language: Greek.

Religion: Eastern Orthodox.

Pindus Mts. run N-S; fertile valleys; tobacco, olives grown; tourist indust.

Powerful city-states from 6th cent. BC; fell to Romans 146 BC; Turkish from 1453; independent 1829; military regime 1967-74; republic 1973.

**Flag:** adopted in 1970, replaced in 1975 by a plain white cross over blue, readopted in 1981; the design dates from *c* 1832, and is said to represent the national motto, 'Liberty or Death'.

**GREENLAND,** isl. of Denmark, in N Atlantic.
Area: 2,176,000 sq km (840,000 sq mi).
Population: 49,666 (1976).
Capital: Godthaab.
Language: Danish.
Religion: Lutheranism.
Largest isl. in the world, mostly covered by icecap; cryolite mining; sheep in SW; cod, halibut fishing indust.
Discovered *c* 982 by Eric the Red; Danish colony until 1953; internal autonomy 1979.
**Flag**: adopted in the early 1980s; the white represents the inland ice and icebergs, the red the sunrise and sunset.


**GRENADA,** isl. state of SE West Indies.
Area: 311 sq km (120 sq mi).
Population: 110,410 (1982).
Capital: St George's.
Language: English.
Religion: Christian.
Produces spices (esp. nutmeg), cocoa, fruit, rum; tourist indust.
British colony from 1783; independent 1974; Marxist coup of 1983 followed by US and Caribbean military invasion; British Commonwealth member.
**Flag**: adopted in 1974; displays the chief product, the nutmeg; the seven stars represent the island's seven parishes, the colours sunshine (gold), agriculture (green), fervour and freedom (red).

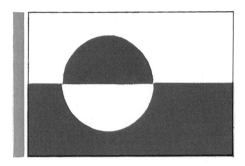

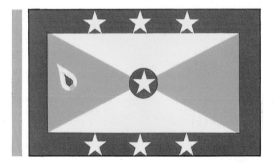

**GUAM,** isl. of W Pacific Ocean.
Area: 540 sq km (210 sq mi).
Population: 105,979 (1980).
Capital: Agaña.
Languages: English, Chamorro.
Religion: Christian.
Subsistence farming; economy dominated by US military base.
Discovered by Magellan 1521; taken from Spain by US 1898; occupied by Japan 1941-4; self-government 1950; US dependency.
**Flag**: adopted in 1917; the emblem displays a palm tree and a golden beach; only flown in conjunction with the US flag.


**GUATEMALA,** republic of Central America.
Area: 108,889 (42,042 sq mi).
Population: 7,500,000 (est. 1984).
Capital: Guatemala City.
Languages: Spanish, Indian dialects.
Religion: Roman Catholic, Protestant.
Volcanic mts.; jungle in N; agric. economy; grows coffee, cotton, bananas.
Maya-Quiche civilizations had declined prior to Spanish conquest 1524; independent 1821; basis of Central American Federation 1825-38; frequent earthquakes.
**Flag**: adopted after 1871 revolution; uses the traditional Central American colours of blue and white arranged vertically.

**GUIANA, FRENCH,** overseas dept. of France, NE South America.
Area: 91,000 sq km (35,135 sq mi).
Population: 73,022 (1982).
Capital: Cayenne.
Language: French.
Religion: Roman Catholic.
Rises from Atlantic coast to tropical forests and mts.; largely undeveloped; exports rum, gold, timber.
Unsuccessful attempt at colonization in 18th cent.; site of former French penal colonies; became French dept. in 1946.
**Flag**: flies the flag of France.

**GUINEA,** republic of W Africa.
Area: 36,130 sq km (13,950 sq mi).
Population: 6,412,000 (est. 1980).
Capital: Conakry.
Language: French.
Religion: Islam.
Humid, marshy coastal plain rises to interior highlands; cattle raising; exports bananas, iron ore, alumina.
Former French Guinea estab. 1895; part of French West Africa from 1904; independent 1958.
**Flag**: adopted in 1958; the design is based on the French tricolour, and uses the Pan-African colours to represent work (red), justice (yellow) and solidarity (green).

**GUINEA-BISSAU,** republic of W Africa.
Area: 36,130 sq km (13,950 sq mi).
Population: 760,000 (est. 1979).
Capital: Bissau.
Language: Portuguese.
Religions: native, Islam.
Coastal mangrove swamp, tropical forest; produces palm oil, hardwoods, copra, groundnuts.
Centre of slave trade 17th-18th cent.; Portuguese colony 1879; independent 1974; coup 1980; claims right to Cape Verde Isls.
**Flag**: adopted in 1974, the flag had been used since 1961 by the liberation movement; uses Pan-African colours, with a black star.


**GUYANA,** state of NE South America.
Area: 215,000 sq km (83,000 sq mi).
Population: 793,000 (est. 1980).
Capital: Georgetown.
Language: English.
Religions: Hinduism, Islam, Christianity.
Mainly jungle with cultivable coastal strip; produces sugar, rice, bauxite.
Settled by Dutch in 17th cent.; British occupation 1796; independent 1966; British Commonwealth member.
**Flag**: adopted in 1966; the colours represent the forests (green), the future (gold), the people's energy (red), their perseverance (black) and the rivers (white).

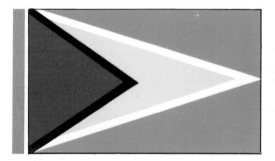

**HAITI,** republic of West Indies.
Area: 27,713 sq km (10,700 sq mi).
Population: 6,000,000 (est. 1984).
Capital: Port-au-Prince.
Languages: French, Creole dialect.
Religion: Roman Catholic.
Largely wooded mts.; tropical climate; subsistence agric.; grows coffee, sugar, sisal, timber, bauxite.
Spanish ceded possession in 17th cent. to French sugar planters; independent 1804; historically ruled by despots, esp. Duvalier (1957-71).
**Flag**: adopted in 1964; the colours, said to represent the country's African heritage, were first used *c* 1804-6.


**HONDURAS,** republic of Central America.
Area: 112,088 sq km (43,277 sq mi).
Population: 3,600,000 (est. 1982).
Capital: Tegucigalpa.
Language: Spanish.
Religion: Roman Catholic.
Humid Caribbean coast; Mosquito Coast in NE; forested mts. in interior with silver mines; US-owned banana plantations.
Colonized by Spanish in 16th cent.; independent 1821; member of Central American Federation 1825-38; disastrous floods in 1974.
**Flag**: the traditional Central American colours were adopted in 1949; the five stars represent the United Provinces of Central America.

**HONG KONG,** British crown colony of SE Asia.
Area: 1034 sq km (398 sq mi).
Population: 5,344,400 (1983).
Capital: Victoria.
Languages: English, Chinese.
Religions: Buddhism, Confucianism, Christian.
Major textile, garment industs.; shipbuilding, electrical goods; free port; important link for Chinese trade.
Occupied by British in 1841; New Territories leased for 99 years from China in 1898; colony will revert to Chinese rule in 1997.
**Flag:** Blue Ensign flown since 1841; the coat of arms dates from 1959, and bears two British lions and a Chinese dragon.

**HUNGARY,** republic of EC Europe.
Area: 93,012 sq km (35,912 sq mi).
Population: 10,710,000 (1980).
Capital: Budapest.
Language: Magyar.
Religions: Roman Catholic, Protestant.
Danube runs N-S; Alfold plain to E; Bakony forest to W; collective agric.; developing industries.
Kingdom estab. 11th cent.; ruled by Ottoman Turks until 1683; part of Hapsburg Empire until 1848 and of Austro-Hungary 1867-1918; Communist govt. estab. 1948; 1956 revolt crushed by USSR.
**Flag:** adopted in 1948; the colours date from the 9th cent.; an emblem representing the People's Republic was added in 1949 and removed after 1956.

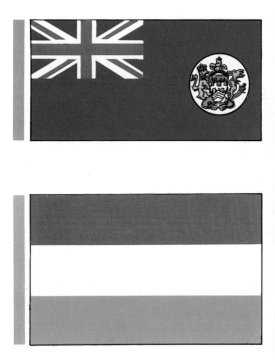

**ICELAND,** isl. republic in N Atlantic.
Area: 102,950 sq km (39,750 sq mi).
Population: 237,894 (1983).
Capital: Reykjavik.
Language: Icelandic.
Religion: Lutheran.
Uninhabited C plateau; active volcanoes, hot springs;
mild, wet climate; fishing, grazing.
Colonized 9th cent. by Norwegians; first parliament
(930) in Europe; united with Denmark 1380-1918;
independent 1944.
**Flag:** adopted in 1918; the traditional colours of blue
and white are a combination of those of Norway and
Denmark.


**INDIA,** republic of SC Asia.
Area: *c* 3,268,000 sq km (1,262,000 sq mi).
Population: 683,880,051 (1981).
Capital: New Delhi.
Languages: Hindi, and 14 official state languages.
Religions: Hinduism, Islam.
Largely plains; Himalayas to N; climate mainly tropical
monsoon; grows rice, cotton, tea, timber.
United under Moguls 16th-18th cent.; East India Co.
rule 1757-1858 transferred to Britain after Indian
Mutiny; independent 1947.
**Flag:** originally the Indian National Congress flag;
orange represents the Hindu majority, green the
Muslims and white peace; the Buddhist wheel was
added on adoption of the flag in 1947.

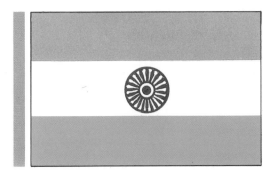

**INDONESIA,** republic of SE Asia.
Area: *c* 1,904,000 sq km (736,000 sq mi).
Population: 157,000,000 (est. 1984).
Capital: Djakarta.
Language: Bahasa Indonesian.
Religion: Islam.
Mainly mountainous; equatorial climate, heavy rainfall; grows rice, rubber, spices; petroleum.
Colonized by Dutch East India Co. in 17th cent.; independence from the Netherlands proclaimed 1945; sovereignty transferred 1949.
**Flag**: flown in 1928, adopted in 1945; the red represents courage, the white justice and purity; the colours have stood for revolt and the struggle for independence since the Middle Ages.

**IRAN,** republic of SW Asia.
Area: 1,648,000 sq km (636,000 sq mi).
Population: 39,190,000 (est. 1982).
Capital: Tehran.
Language: Persian.
Religions: Islam, Zoroastrian, Bahai, Christian.
C plateau surrounded by mts. in N, S, and E; produces wool, rice, cotton; great oil resources.
Persian empire fell to Alexander *c* 330 BC; Pahlevi dynasty founded 1925; Shah exiled and Islamic republic estab. 1979; war with Iraq began in 1980.
**Flag**: the tricolour was adopted in 1907; the symbol combining the words 'There is no God but Allah' and the text proclaiming God's greatness were added after the founding of the republic.

**IRAQ,** republic of SW Asia.
Area: *c* 435,000 sq km (168,000 sq mi).
Population: *c* 14,000,000 (est. 1984).
Capital: Baghdad.
Languages: Arabic, Kurdish.
Religion: Islam.
Drained by the Tigris and Euphrates; mountainous N rich in oil; cotton and dates grown in SE.
Ottoman domination until WWI; kingdom 1921-58; became republic after military coup; war with Iran began in 1980.
**Flag**: adopted in 1963; uses the Pan-Arab colours; the three stars represent the then hoped-for unity between Iraq, Syria and Egypt.


**IRELAND, Republic of,** S part of isl. of W Europe.
Area: *c* 70,000 sq km (27,000 sq mi).
Population: 3,443,405 (1981).
Capital: Dublin.
Languages: Irish, English.
Religion: Roman Catholic.
Mainly agric., esp. dairying; fishing; tourism.
Struggle for independence from UK ended with partition of N and S and estab. of Irish Free State 1921; republic proclaimed 1949; left British Commonwealth.
**Flag**: dates from 1848, adopted in 1920; green represents the Catholics, and orange the Protestants; the white stands for peace between the two.

**ISRAEL,** republic of SW Asia, on Mediterranean.
Area: *c* 21,000 sq km (8100 sq mi).
Population: 3,921,700 (est. 1980).
Capital: Jerusalem.
Language: Hebrew.
Religion: Judaism.
Fertile coastal plain (citrus fruit), rises in N to Galilee (grain); irrigated desert in S.
Part of hist. Palestine; occupied by Romans (70 BC-AD 636), Ottomans (1516-1917); British mandate (1920-1948) ended in estab. of Jewish state in 1948; territ. wars with Arab states from 1948.
**Flag:** adopted in 1948 from a late 1800s design; the Star of David is between the blue and white stripes of the Hebrew prayer shawl.

**ITALY,** republic of S Europe.
Area: 301,165 sq km (116,280 sq mi).
Population: 56,830,000 (1983).
Capital: Rome.
Language: Italian.
Religion: Roman Catholic.
Alps in N, fertile Po basin in NE, Apennines run NW-SE; fruit, wine, olives; major tourist indust.
Settled by Etruscans, Greeks; Roman Empire *c* 5th cent. BC - 5th cent. AD; divided into many small states until unification in 1861; republic from 1946 after defeat of Fascist regime in WWII.
**Flag:** adopted in 1861; thought to derive from the standard of the French Guard in Napoleon's invasion of 1796.

**IVORY COAST,** republic of W Africa.
Area: 322,500 sq km (124,500 sq mi).
Population: 7,000,000 (est. 1979).
Capital: Abidjan.
Language: French.
Religions: native, Islam.
Savannah in N, tropical forest in C, coastal swamps in S; produces cotton, coffee, bananas, hardwoods; former centre of ivory, slave trade.
French colony from 1893; part of French West Africa from 1904; independent in 1960.
**Flag**: adopted in 1959; as with many former French colonies, the national flag is based on that of France.


**JAMAICA,** isl. state of West Indies.
Area: 10,962 sq km (4232 sq mi).
Population: 2,265,400 (est. 1982).
Capital: Kingston.
Language: English.
Religion: Protestant.
Mts. in E; tropical climate; grows sugar cane, fruit, spices, tobacco; exports bauxite; tourism.
Settled by Spanish in 16th cent.; captured by English in 1655; slavery abolished 1833; indpendent 1962; republic 1980; British Commonwealth member.
**Flag**: adopted in 1962; the gold represents natural resources and the sun, the green agriculture and the future, the black hardships.

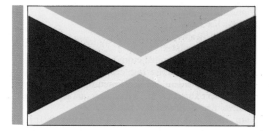

**JAPAN,** isl. kingdom of E Asia.
Area: *c* 372,000 sq km (142,000 sq mi).
Population: 118,390,000 (1982).
Capital: Tokyo.
Language: Japanese.
Religions: Shinto, Buddhism.
Mts., active volcanoes; frequent earthquakes; monsoon climate; rice, cereals, soya beans, major fisheries.
Feudal society under shoguns until 19th cent.; world power after defeating China (1895), Russia (1905); imperial power curtailed after defeat in WWII.
**Flag**: adopted in 1870, the red sun represents the 'land of the rising sun'; emperors had used the symbol for centuries to represent Japanese power.


**JORDAN,** kingdom of SW Asia.
Area: *c* 98,400 sq km (38,000 sq mi).
Population: 2,400,000 (est. 1984).
Capital: Amman.
Language: Arabic.
Religion: Sunni Islam.
Mts., arid desert; limited cultivation (wheat, fruit).
Part of Ottoman empire 16th cent.-1918; mandated to Britain; independent 1946; defeated by Israelis (1967) who occupied part of W Jordan; incl. an est. 950,000 refugees and displaced persons.
**Flag**: the Pan-Arab colours were adopted in 1921; the seven-pointed star represents the opening verses of the Koran.

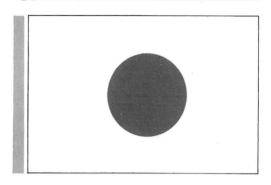

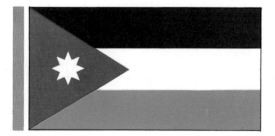

**KAMPUCHEA,** state of SE Asia.
Area: *c* 181,300 sq km (70,000 sq mi).
Population: 6,000,000 (est. 1981).
Capital: Phnom Penh.
Language: Khmer.
Religion: Hinayana Buddhism.
Large plain drained by Mekong; mainly agric. (rice); fisheries.
Formerly French protect. 1863-1955; monarchy 1955; republic estab. 1970; Khmer Rouge victory (1975) in civil war; regime overthrown by Vietnamese-backed rebels in 1979; formerly known as Cambodia.
**Flag**: adopted in 1979; the red is traditionally Kampuchean as well as Communist, and all regimes have featured the Angkor Wat temple on the flag.

**KENYA,** republic of E Africa.
Area: 583,000 sq km (225,000 sq mi).
Population: 17,000,000 (est. 1984).
Capital: Nairobi.
Languages: Swahili, English.
Religions: native, Christian.
Coastal strip, arid plains in N, highlands in W; produces coffee, tea, grain, cattle; game reserves; unexploited minerals.
Coastal strip leased by UK from Zanzibar 1887; protect./crown colony from 1920; independent 1963; republic 1964; British Commonwealth member.
**Flag**: adopted in 1963; based on the African National Union party flag; the masai shield and crossed spears represent defence of freedom.

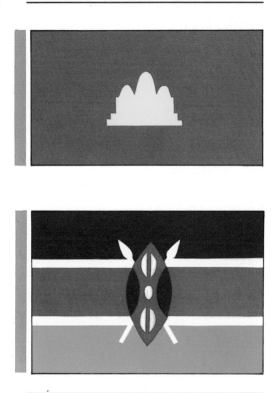

**KIRIBATI,** isl. state of WC Pacific Ocean.
Area: 655 sq km (253 sq mi).
Population: 60,000 (est. 1982).
Capital: Tarawa.
Language: English.
Religion: Christian.
Produces copra, phosphates; fishing, tourist industries.
Formerly known as Gilbert Isls.; as part of Gilbert and
Ellice Isls. was British protect. from 1892, colony 1915;
split from Ellice Isls. (Tuvalu) 1978; independent 1979.
**Flag:** adopted in 1979; displays a frigate bird flying over
the sun as it rises over the Pacific Ocean.

**KOREA, NORTH,** republic of E Asia.
Area: *c* 120,500 sq km (47,000 sq mi).
Population: 18,000,000 (est. 1982).
Capital: Pyongyang.
Language: Korean.
Religion: Confucianism.
Mts., forests; gold, iron deposits.
Kingdom (with South Korea) 1392-1910 until Japanese
annexation; liberation after WWII led to Russian
occupation of N until 1948; Communist republic estab.
1948; Korean War 1950-3.
**Flag:** adopted in 1948; the colours are those of the
traditional Korean standard, but in a new Communist
pattern with a red star.

**KOREA, SOUTH,** republic of E Asia.
Area: *c* 98,500 sq km (38,000 sq mi).
Population: *c* 39,000,000 (est. 1982).
Capital: Seoul.
Language: Korean.
Religion: Confucianism.
Mountainous; grows rice, barley; tungsten, coal.
Kingdom (with North Korea) 1392-1910 until Japanese
annexation; liberation after WWII led to US occupation
of S until 1949; republic estab. 1948; Korean War
1950-3.
**Flag:** adopted in 1950; the white represents peace, the
yin-yang nature's opposing forces; the black symbols
represent the four seasons, the compass point, and the
sun, moon, earth and heaven.


**KUWAIT,** independent sheikdom of SW Asia, at head of
Persian Gulf.
Area: *c* 18,000 sq km (6950 sq mi).
Population: 1,786,616 (1984).
Capital: Al-Kuwait.
Language: Arabic.
Religion: Islam.
Mainly desert; major oil producer.
Formerly nominal part of Ottoman Empire; British
protect. 1899-1961; independence under British pro-
tect. recognized 1914; shares control of Neutral Terri-
tory with Saudi Arabia.
**Flag:** the Pan-Arab colours of red, white, black and
green were adopted in 1961.

**LAOS,** republic of SE Asia.
Area: *c* 236,000 sq km (91,500 sq mi).
Population: 3,000,000 (est. 1976).
Capital: Vientiane.
Languages: Laotian, French.
Religion: Buddhism.
Forested, mountainous terrain apart from Mekong valley; grows rice, maize, tobacco, coffee.
French protect. 1893-1949; civil war from 1960; North Vietnamese forces involved from 1967; monarchy abolished and Communist govt. estab.1975.
**Flag:** adopted in 1975; the blue represents the Mekong river, the white disc the moon, the red the unity and purpose of the people.


**LEBANON,** republic of SW Asia, on Mediterranean.
Area: *c* 10,000 sq km (3860 sq mi).
Population: 2,780,000 (est. 1984).
Capital: Beirut.
Language: Arabic.
Religions: Islam, Maronite Christian.
Fertile Beqa valley (grain, fruit) lies between Lebanon Mts. and Anti-Lebanon range to E.
Centre of ancient Phoenician empire; part of Syria under Romans, Byzantines and Turks until French mandate 1920; independent 1943; religious and civil strife from mid-70s onward.
**Flag:** adopted in 1943, the colours are those of the Lebanese Legion in WWI; the cedar tree has been a Lebanese symbol since Biblical times.

**LESOTHO,** kingdom of S Africa, surrounded by Republic of South Africa.

Area: 30,300 sq km (11,700 sq mi).

Population: 1,204,000 (est. 1981).

Capital: Maseru.

Languages: Sesotho, English.

Religions: native, Christian.

Mts. in E, elsewhere tableland; stock rearing; exports wool, mohair, diamonds.

British protect. of Basutoland from 1868; independent 1966; British Commonwealth member.

**Flag**: adopted in 1966; the blue represents rain, the red faith in the future, and green the land; the central emblem is a traditional conical woven hat.

**LIBERIA,** republic of W Africa.

Area: 111,300 sq km (43,000 sq mi).

Population: 1,481,524 (1974).

Capital: Monrovia.

Languages: tribal, English.

Religions: native, Christian.

Coastal plain, inland plateaux; extensive rain forest; rice grown; exports iron ore, gold, rubber; 'flag of convenience' merchant fleet.

Founded 1822 as colony for freed American slaves; independent republic from 1847.

**Flag**: adopted in 1847; based on the Stars and Stripes, but has 11 stripes and a single white 5-pointed star.

**LIBYA,** republic of N Africa.
Area: 1,759,500 sq km (679,350 sq mi).
Population: 3,100,000 (est. 1981).
Capital: Tripoli.
Language: Arabic.
Religion: Islam.
Fertile coastal strip, interior mainly desert; grows grain, fruit; major oil and gas producer.
Under Turkish rule from 16th cent.; taken by Italy 1912; Franco-British military govt. in WWII; kingdom estab. 1951; republic under Qadhafi after 1969 coup; 'direct democracy' introduced 1977.
**Flag:** adopted in 1977; the plain green represents the nation's Islamic faith and the agricultural revolution.


**LIECHTENSTEIN,** principality of WC Europe, between Austria and Switzerland.
Area: 166 sq km (64 sq mi).
Population: 26,512 (1983).
Capital: Vaduz.
Language: German.
Religion: Roman Catholic.
Cereals, wine; tourism.
Created 1719 from union of Vaduz and Schellenberg countships; independent 1866; joined Swiss Customs Union 1923.
**Flag:** the colours date back to the early 19th cent.; the gold crown was added in 1937 to avoid confusion with the flag flown by Haiti at that time.

**LUXEMBOURG,** grand duchy of NW Europe.

Area: 2587 sq km (999 sq mi).

Population: 365,500 (1983).

Capital: Luxembourg.

Language: Letzeburgesch (German dialect).

Religion: Roman Catholic.

Agric., cattle; iron mining.

Duchy from 1354 (Hapsburg from 15th cent.); grand duchy within Netherlands from 1815; independent 1890; in Benelux Customs Union from 1948.

**Flag**: similar colours to that of the Netherlands, but the flag is longer and the blue lighter; colours taken from the Grand Duke's 13th-cent. coat of arms.


**MADAGASCAR,** isl. republic of W Indian Ocean.

Area: 587,000 sq km (226,600 sq mi).

Population: 9,000,000 (est. 1984).

Capital: Tananarive.

Languages: Malagasy, French.

Religions: Christian, native.

Narrow coastal strip; C highlands; grows sugar, coffee, rice; cattle raising; unique flora and fauna.

French colony from 1896; autonomous republic 1958; independent 1960; known as Malagasy Republic 1958-75.

**Flag**: adopted in 1958; the red and white traditionally represent the Hova people, the green the inhabitants of the coast; the colours are said to have been brought by the Hova from SE Asia.

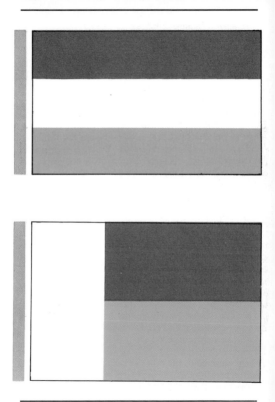

**MALAWI,** republic of EC Africa.
Area: *c* 118,000 sq km (45,250 sq mi).
Population: 5,547,460 (1977).
Capital: Lilongwe.
Languages: Bantu dialects, English.
Religions: native, Christian.
Great Rift Valley runs N-S, filled by Lake Malawi; elsewhere plateau, incl. highlands in SW; produces tea, cotton, tobacco, sugar, groundnuts.
British protect. estab. 1891; called Nyasaland 1907-64; independent 1964; republic 1966; British Commmwealth member.
**Flag**: adopted in 1964; uses the Malawi Congress Party colours; black represents liberation, and the rising sun the new era.

**MALAYSIA,** federated state of SE Asia, incl. S Malay penin., N Borneo.
Area: *c* 332,650 sq km (128,500 sq mi).
Population: 13,435,588 (1980).
Capital: Kuala Lumpur.
Language: Malayan, English.
Religion: Islam.
Interior mts. flanked by plains; densely forested; equatorial climate; major rubber, tin producer.
Part of the Federation of Malaya 1948-63; independent 1957; Singapore seceded 1965; British Commonwealth member.
**Flag**: adopted in 1963; the 14 stripes and points of the star represent the 13 states and Kuala Lumpur; the crescent and star are Islamic symbols.

**MALDIVE ISLANDS,** republic in N Indian Ocean, SW of Sri Lanka.
Area: 298 sq km mi (115 sq mi).
Population: 160,200 (1982).
Capital: Malé.
Language: Divehi.
Religion: Islam.
Coral atoll isl. chain consisting of *c* 2,000 isls.; agric. economy based on coconuts, fruit; tourism.
British protect. from 1887; independent 1965; republic 1968; British Commonwealth member.
**Flag:** adopted in 1965; originally plain red, an Islamic green panel with white crescent was added early this century.


**MALI,** republic of W Africa.
Area: 1,240,000 sq km. (478,000).
Population: 7,160,000 (est. 1981).
Capital: Bamako.
Languages: French, various African.
Religions: Islam, native.
Desert in N, elsewhere semidesert; marsh in SW; grows maize, groundnuts, cotton, rice; cattle raising; economy severely affected by drought.
Occupied by France in late 19th cent.; colony from 1904; part of Mali Federation (1959-60) with Senegal; independent 1960.
**Flag:** adopted in 1960; uses the Pan-African colours arranged in the form of the flag of France.

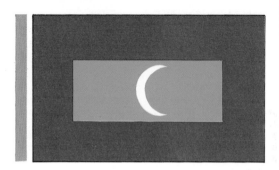

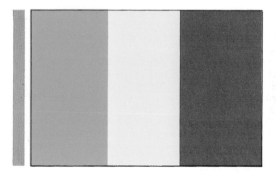

**MALTA,** republic of S Europe, in Mediterranean Sea.
Area: 316 sq km (122 sq mi).
Population: 341,000 (est. 1981).
Capital: Valletta.
Languages: Maltese, English.
Religion: Roman Catholic.
Tourist resort; agric. incl. cereals, potatoes, fruit.
Taken by Norman Sicily 1090; given to Knights Hospitallers 1530; annexed by Britain 1814; independent 1964; British Commonwealth member.
**Flag**: adopted in 1964; the colours are of great antiquity, from the arms of the Knights of St John; the George Cross was added in 1943 after the award of that medal to the island for its heroism.


**MARIANAS, NORTHERN,** state of W Pacific Ocean.
Area: 476 sq km (184 sq mi).
Population: 16,780 (1980)
Administrative centre: Garapan.
Languages: Malayo-Polynesian dialects, English.
Religion: Christian.
Produces copra, sugar cane.
Placed under US administration by UN in 1947; separated from Trust Territory of the Pacific Islands in 1976; autonomous US Commonwealth.
**Flag**: displays a chalice-shaped stone symbol (a Polynesian 'taga') bearing a white star, on a field of UN blue.

**MAURITANIA,** republic of NW Africa.
Area: 1,031,000 sq km (398,000 sq mi).
Population: 1,634,000 (est. 1980).
Capital: Nouakchott.
Languages: Arabic, French.
Religion: Islam.
Mainly in Sahara; pop. mostly nomadic herdsmen; limited agric. (maize, millet); exports iron and copper ore, gum arabic, dried fish.
French protect. from 1903; colony from 1920; independent 1960.
**Flag**: adopted in 1959; the star and crescent represent the dominance of Islam and the country's official name, the Mauritanian Islamic Republic.


**MAURITIUS,** isl. state of W Indian Ocean.
Area: 1860 sq km (720 sq mi).
Population: 949,686 (1982).
Capital: Port Louis.
Languages: English, French.
Religions: Hindu, Christian.
Hilly, largely volcanic; grows sugar cane, tea, tobacco.
Discovered by Portuguese 1505; held successively by Dutch and French, by British from 1815; independent 1968; British Commonwealth member.
**Flag**: adopted in 1968; red represents the independence struggle, blue the Indian Ocean, yellow the bright future, and green the vegetation.

**MEXICO,** republic of SW North America.
Area: 1,972,544 sq km (761,600 sq mi).
Population: 76,800,000 (est. 1984).
Capital: Mexico City.
Languages: Spanish, Indian dialects.
Religion: Roman Catholic.
High C plateau; varied climate; limited agric. in irrigated region; minerals include silver, lead, iron, coal; tourism.
Spanish conquest 1519; independence struggle 1810-21; war with US 1846-8; revolution 1910; civil war estab. new constitution in 1917.
**Flag:** adopted in 1968; the emblem depicts the legendary founding of Mexico City and is an old Aztec symbol; the colours date back to 1821.


**MICRONESIA, Federated States of,** state of W Pacific Ocean.
Area: 1080 sq km (420 sq mi).
Population: 116,662 (1980).
Languages: Malayo-Polynesian dialects, English.
Religion: Christian.
Consists of Pohnpei, Truk, Yap, Kosrae, isls. of the Southern Marianas; exports copra.
Placed under US administration by UN in 1947; Federation formed 1979; fully self-governing incl. foreign affairs, but US responsible for defence.
**Flag:** based on the Trust Territory flag adopted on UN day 1962, the four stars represent the four territories on a field of UN blue.

**MONACO,** principality of S Europe.
Area: 1.5 sq km (0.6 sq mi).
Population: 28,000 (1983).
Capital: Monaco-ville.
Language: French.
Religion: Roman Catholic.
Tourism in Monte Carlo.
Ruled by Grimaldi family from 13th cent.; ruled successively by France (1793-1814), Sardinia (1815-61); constitutional monarchy 1911-59 (restored 1962); customs union with France.
**Flag**: adopted in 1881; the colours derive from the Prince of Monaco's coat of arms, which are of medieval origin.


**MONGOLIA,** republic of C Asia.
Area: *c* 1,566,000 sq km (605,000 sq mi).
Population: 1,820,400 (est. 1984).
Capital: Ulan Bator.
Language: Mongolian.
Religion: Lamaist Buddhism.
High plateau with Gobi Desert in S; extremes of climate; stock rearing; mineral extraction.
Nomadic Mongols conquered region under Genghis Khan *c* 1205; Chinese province from 1691; independent republic estab. 1924.
**Flag**: adopted in 1949; the red represents victory and Communism, the blue patriotism, the gold star endurance and the Communist Party; the *soyombo* symbol under the star represents freedom.

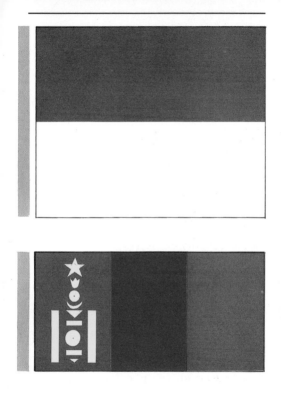

**MONTSERRAT,** isl. of E West Indies.
Area: 98 sq km (38 sq mi).
Population: 12,073 (1980).
Capital: Plymouth.
Language: English.
Religion: Christian.
Volcanic and rugged; subject to earth tremors; exports cotton, fruit, flour bags; tourism.
Discovered by Columbus in 1493; Irish settlement in 1632; taken by France in 1667 and 1782; assigned to Britain in 1783.
**Flag**: the shield on the Blue Ensign displays the Passion cross held by a female figure in green, and dates back to 1909.

**MOROCCO,** kingdom of NW Africa.
Area: 447,000 sq km (172,500 sq mi).
Population: 20,419,555 (1982).
Capital: Rabat.
Language: Arabic.
Religion: Islam.
Largely desert; Atlas Mts. run SW-NE; fertile coast; produces cereals, fruit, olives, cattle; minerals incl. petroleum, phosphates, iron ore.
Berber dynasties 11th-14th cents.; settled by Portuguese 1415-1769; French, Spanish protects. estab. 1912; independent 1956.
**Flag**: adopted in 1956; a plain red flag has been flown since the 16th cent.; the green Seal of Solomon was added in 1915.

**MOZAMBIQUE,** republic of SE Africa.

Area: 783,000 sq km (302,300 sq mi).

Population: 12,000,000 (est. 1982).

Capital: Maputo.

Languages: Bantu, Portuguese.

Religions: native, Christian.

Coastal lowlands, mts.; produces sugar cane, tea.

Became Portuguese East Africa colony in 1907; independent People's Republic formed in 1975.

**Flag**: adopted in 1975, design altered in 1983; the colours and symbols represent agriculture (green, the hoe ), the people (black), mineral wealth (yellow), peace (white), the independence struggle (red, the rifle), education (the book), internationalism (the yellow star).


**NAURU,** isl. republic of SW Pacific Ocean.

Area: 20 sq km (8sq mi).

Population: 7,254 (1977).

Language: Malayo-Polynesian, English.

Religion: Nauruan Protestant, Roman Catholic.

Extensive phosphate deposits (may be exhausted by end of 20th cent.); fertile coastal belt.

Discovered 1798, named Pleasant Isl.; admin. by Australia from 1947 until independence in 1968; British Commonwealth member.

**Flag**: adopted in 1968; the star's 12 points represent the island's 12 tribes, and its position beneath the gold band shows the island's position just south of the Equator.

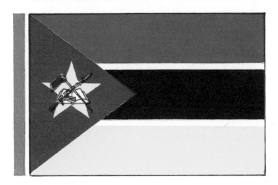

**NEPAL,** kingdom of SC Asia.
Area: *c* 140,000 sq km (54,600 sq mi).
Population: 16,000,000 (est. 1984).
Capital: Katmandu.
Language: Nepali.
Religions: Hinduism, Buddhism.
Formerly remote region in Himalayas, bounded by India and Tibet; rice and grain grown.
Under Gurkha control from 1768; sovereignty recognized by Britain in 1923.
**Flag**: adopted in 1962; the only national flag that is not rectangular in shape; the two separate pennants displaying the crescent moon and sun were first joined in the 19th cent.


**NETHERLANDS,** kingdom of NW Europe.
Area: 41,344 sq km (15,963 sq mi).
Population: 14,394,589 (est. 1984).
Capital: Amsterdam.
Language: Dutch.
Religions: Protestant, Roman Catholic.
Low-lying; large reclaimed areas; dairying, bulbs, fishing; extensive canal system; industs. centred in Amsterdam, Rotterdam, Utrecht.
Part of Low Countries until 16th cent.; rebelled against Spanish rule; independent 1579; estab. overseas empire; union with Belgium 1814-30.
**Flag**: in mid-17th cent., the orange stripe on William of Orange's flag was replaced with a red one, and the tricolour became a symbol of liberty.

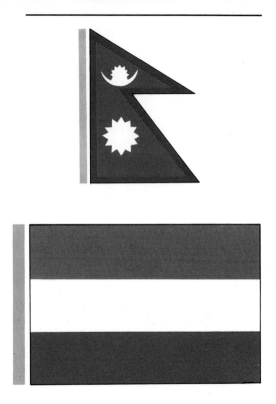

**NETHERLANDS ANTILLES,** two isl. groups in Caribbean.

Area: 394 sq km (1020 sq mi).

Population: 253,234 (est. 1984).

Capital: Willemstad.

Language: Dutch.

Religion: Christian.

N group in Leeward Isls. incl. Saba, St Eustatius, S part of St Martin; S group N of Venezuela incl. Curaçao, Aruba, Bonaire; economy depends on refining of Venezuelan oil.

Dutch territ. from 17th cent.; granted full autonomy in 1954.

**Flag**: adopted in 1959; uses the Netherlands colours; the six stars represent the six islands.


**NEW ZEALAND,** dominion of SW Pacific Ocean.

Area: 268,100 sq km (103,500 sq mi).

Population: 2,379,500 (est. 1983)

Capital: Wellington.

Language: English.

Religion: Christian.

Comprises North, South, and smaller isls.; mt. ranges run NE-SW; fertile valleys; sheep farming, dairying; timber; engineering in towns.

Maori ancestors arrived 10th cent.; under UK rule from 1840; dominion from 1907; independent 1931; British Commonwealth member.

**Flag**: designed in 1869 and adopted in 1917; displays four of the five Southern Cross stars on the Blue Ensign.

**NICARAGUA**, republic of Central America.
Area: 128,410 sq km (49,579 sq mi).
Population: 2,700,000 (est. 1980).
Capital: Managua.
Language: Spanish.
Religion: Roman Catholic.
Mt. ranges and interior plateaus flanked by Pacific, Caribbean coasts; grows cotton, coffee, sugar; exports timber, gold.
Under Spanish rule 1522-1821; member of Central American Federation 1825-38; Somoza dictatorship 1936-79 overthrown by Sandinista revolutionaries.
**Flag**: dates from 1908; uses the traditional Central American colours; apart from having a darker blue, identical with that of El Salvador.

**NIGER**, republic of West Africa.
Area: 1,267,000 sq km (489,000 sq mi).
Population: 5,310,000 (est. 1980).
Capital: Niamey.
Language: French.
Religion: Islam.
Sahara desert, mts. in N, semidesert in S; drained by R. Niger; produces groundnuts, cotton, uranium.
Territ. of French West Africa from 1904; independent 1960.
**Flag**: adopted in 1959; the orange disc represents the sun, the orange stripe the Sahara, the white goodness and purity (and the R. Niger), the green the grass of the south.

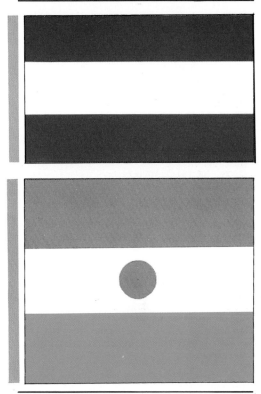

**NIGERIA,** federal republic of W Africa.
Area: 925,000 sq km (357,000 sq mi).
Population: 55,654,000 (1983).
Capital: Lagos.
Languages: Hausa, Ibo, Yoruba, English.
Religions: Islam, Christian, animism.
Semi-desert in N, savannah plateaux in C, tropical forest in S; main rivers Niger, Benue; produces palm oil, cocoa, groundnuts, cotton, petroleum.
Colony and protect. estab.1914; independent 1960; republic 1963; attempted secession of Biafra caused civil war 1967-70; British Commonwealth member.
**Flag:** adopted in 1960; the green represents the country's forests, the white peace.


**NIUE,** isl. of SC Pacific Ocean, between Tonga and Cook Isls.
Area: 260 sq km (100 sq mi).
Population: 3,002 (1983).
Capital: Alofi.
Language: English.
Religion: Christian.
Produces fruit, copra.
Administered by New Zealand from 1901; internal self-government from 1974.
**Flag:** adopted in 1975; the bright yellow is said to represent warmth towards New Zealand and the British Commonwealth.

**NORWAY,** kingdom of NW Europe.
Area: 324,250 sq km (125,200 sq mi).
Population: 4,106,651 (est. 1983).
Capital: Oslo.
Language: Norwegian.
Religion: Lutheran.
Deeply indented coast; mountainous; partly within Arctic Circle; North Sea fishing, forestry, minerals, offshore oil resources, h.e.p.
Early history dominated by Vikings; united with Denmark 1397-1814, and with Sweden 1397-1523; independent from 1905.
**Flag:** adopted in 1821, the flag was not generally used until 1898; based on the flag of Denmark.


**OMAN,** sultanate of SW Asia, SE Arabian penin., along Gulf of Oman.
Area: *c* 212,000 sq km (82,000 sq mi).
Population: 850,000 (1982).
Capital: Muscat.
Language: Arabic.
Religion: Islam.
Coastal plain backed by mts., arid plateau; fishing; exports dates, limes, pomegranates, petroleum.
Called Muscat and Oman until 1970; linked by treaty with UK.
**Flag:** adopted in 1970; the state arms of swords and a dagger with stripes of white and green are placed upon the traditional Omani red field.

**PAKISTAN,** republic of SC Asia.
Area: *c* 804,000 sq km (311,000 sq mi).
Population: 83,780,000 (est. 1981).
Capital: Islamabad.
Language: Urdu.
Religion: Islam.
Mts. in N and W, plains watered by Indus, desert in SW; grows grains, rice, cotton.
Created 1947 on Indian independence, following Moslem agitation; republic 1956; war with India over Kashmir 1965; civil war with East Pakistan led to the latter's independence as Bangladesh.
**Flag**: adopted in 1947; Islamic green with the Muslim crescent and star, and a white stripe to represent other religions and minorities.

**PANAMA,** republic of Central America.
Area: 75,650 sq km (29,210 sq mi).
Population: 1,940,000 (est. 1980).
Capital: Panama City.
Language: Spanish.
Religion: Roman Catholic.
Volcanic mts. in E and W; fertile lowlands in C; grows bananas, coffee, mahogany; fishing.
Explored by Balboa 1513; part of Colombia after break with Spain 1821; independence in 1903 after Colombia's refusal to allow US to build canal.
**Flag**: adopted in 1903; blue represents the Conservatives, red the Liberals, white the hope of peace; the red star stands for law and order, the blue star public honesty.

**PAPUA NEW GUINEA,** state of SW Pacific.
Area: 463,000 sq km (178,000 sq mi).
Population: 3,160,000 (est. 1983).
Capital: Port Moresby.
Languages: English, many native languages.
Religions: native, Christian.
Timber exports; minerals incl. gold, copper.
Formed from Australian territ. of Papua and former German colony of New Guinea, mandated to Australia 1920; independent 1975; British Commonwealth member.
**Flag**: adopted in 1971; the Papuan bird of paradise is depicted in gold on the red, and the Australian stars of the Southern Cross constellation in white on the black.


**PARAGUAY,** republic of SC South America.
Area: 406,752 sq km (157,047 sq mi).
Population: 3,026,165 (1982).
Capital: Asunción.
Languages: Spanish, Guarani.
Religion: Roman Catholic.
Unexploited plains in W; pop. and indust. concentrated between Paraguay and Paraná rivers; cotton; cattle rearing (meat packing).
Settled by Spanish 16th cent.; independent 1811; extended frontier in Chaco war with Bolivia 1932-5.
**Flag**: adopted in 1842, the obverse displays the May Star, representing liberation from Spain, while the reverse displays the Treasury Seal; the only differing obverse/reverse national flag.

**PERU,** republic of W South America.
Area: 1,285,210 sq km (496,220 sq mi).
Population: 14,121,564 (1972).
Capital: Lima.
Languages: Spanish, Quechua, Aymará.
Religion: Roman Catholic.
Pacific coastal plain rises to Andean ranges in interior; minerals incl. zinc, silver, copper; cotton; sheep, llaamas, alpacas; fishing.
Inca empire destroyed by Spanish after 1532; revolutionary war 1821-24; independent 1824.
**Flag**: adopted in 1825; red and white are said to have been chosen as the national colours after a flock of flamingos flew over the revolutionary troops in 1820.


**PHILIPPINES,** republic of SE Asia.
Area: *c* 300,000 sq km (115,000 sq mi).
Population: 48,098,460 (est. 1980).
Capital: Manila.
Language: Filipino.
Religion: Roman Catholic, Islam.
Mountainous, densely forested; tropical monsoon climate; produces rice, corn, hemp, sugar, timber; minerals incl. chromite, gold.
Under Spanish control 1564-1898 until ceded to US after Spanish-American War; independent 1946.
**Flag**: dates back to 1890s, adopted in 1946; the eight rays of the sun represent the eight provinces that revolted against Spanish rule in 1898, and the stars represent the three main island groups.

**POLAND,** republic of EC Europe.
Area: *c* 312,600 sq km (120,700 sq mi).
Population: 36,400,000 (1982).
Capital: Warsaw.
Language: Polish.
Religion: Roman Catholic.
Forested N, Carpathians in S, elsewhere fertile plain; cereals, livestock; indust. incl. coal, iron, lead mining, textile mfg., engineering.
First united 10th cent.; partitioned many times between the major powers; independent again after WWI; Communist govt. estab. 1947.
**Flag**: adopted in 1919; the red and white derive from the 13th-cent. emblem, a white eagle on a red field.


**POLYNESIA, FRENCH,** isl. group of S Pacific Ocean.
Area: 4,000 sq mi (1,550 sq km).
Population: 148,000 (est. 1983).
Capital: Papetee (in Tahiti).
Languages: French, Polynesian.
Religion: Roman Catholic.
Comprises Gambier, Marquesas, Society, Tuamotu, Tubuai archipelagos; produces copra, coffee, vanilla, citrus fruits, pearls; tourism.
Acquired by France in 19th cent.; known as French Oceania until 1958; internal autonomy 1984.
**Flag**: adopted in 1984; red and white have been used in Tahitian flags since 1820; the figures on the pirogue represent the five island groups, the sun the life and abundance of the sea.

**PORTUGAL,** republic of SW Europe.

Area: 92,000 sq km (35,500 sq mi).

Population: 9,862,700 (est. 1979).

Capital: Lisbon.

Language: Portuguese.

Religion: Roman Catholic.

Mts. in N, E; agric., wine, cork, fishing; subtropical in S (tourism).

Independent from 12th cent.; overseas empire founded 15th-16th cent.; Spanish rule 1580-1668; republic estab. 1910; Salazar dictatorship 1932-68.

**Flag**: adopted in 1910; the red represents the blood shed in the independence struggle against Spain, the green the sea; the armillary shield symbolizes Portugal's lead in exploration.


**PUERTO RICO,** US isl. territ. of E West Indies.

Area: 8871 sq km (3425 sq mi).

Population: 3,196,520 (1980).

Capital: San Juan.

Languages: Spanish, English.

Religion: Roman Catholic.

Mainly mountainous; tropical climate; fertile agric. soil (sugar cane, tobacco).

Settled by Spanish 1508; ceded to US after 1898 war; became 'Commonwealth' 1952; much emigration to US because of unemployment.

**Flag**: adopted in 1952; dates from the revolutionary movement of 1895; only flown with the Stars and Stripes; based on the flag of Cuba.

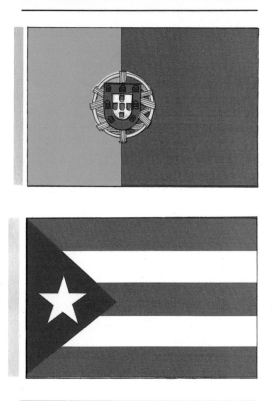

**QATAR,** penin. of E Arabia, in Persian Gulf.
Area: *c* 11,400 sq km (4400 sq mi).
Population: 250,000 (est. 1982).
Capital: Doha.
Language: Arabic.
Religion: Islam.
Oil reserves; some semi-nomadic tribesmen.
Sheikdom under British protection until 1971; allied
with United Arab Emirates; see also Bahrain.
**Flag:** dates back to mid-19th cent., adopted in 1971;
some authorities claim that the maroon colour results
from the natural effect of the sun on the traditional red
banner.


**ROMANIA,** republic of SE Europe.
Area: 237,428 sq km (91,671 sq mi).
Population: 22,480,000 (1982).
Capital: Bucharest.
Language: Romanian.
Religion: Eastern Orthodox.
Crossed N-S by Carpathians, E-W by Transylvanian
Alps; agric. mainly grains, livestock, vines; indust.
development rapid, esp. petroleum.
Formed by union of Moldavia, Wallachia 1859; inde-
pendent 1878; Communist govt. estab. 1948.
**Flag:** adopted in 1948, amended in 1965; the colours are
Moldavian and Wallachian, and the coat of arms
displays the country's natural resources, topped by a
Communist star.

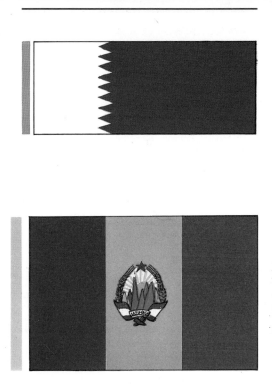

**RWANDA,** republic of EC Africa.
Area: 26,400 sq km (10,200 sq mi).
Population: 5,100,000 (1981).
Capital: Kigali.
Languages: Bantu, French.
Religions: native, French.
Mainly high plateau, Lake Kivu in W; cattle rearing; tin mining; exports coffee.
Former kingdom, part of German East Africa from 1899; part of Belgian colony of Ruanda-Urundi after WWI; independent republic 1962; massacre of Tutsi population 1964.
**Flag:** adopted in 1962; uses the Pan-African colours with an 'R' in the centre to distinguish it from the flag of Guinea.

**St HELENA,** isl. of S Atlantic.
Area: 122 sq km (47 sq mi).
Population: 5,499 (1982).
Capital: Jamestown.
Language: English.
Religion: Christian.
Volcanic origin; numerous rugged mts.; limited land and sea resources.
British possession from 17th cent.; Napoleon's final place of exile 1815-21; British crown colony from 1834; Ascension and Tristan da Cunha are dependencies.
**Flag:** the Blue Ensign displays a trading ship flying the flag of St George, between two volcanic rocks.

**St KITTS-NEVIS,** state of E West Indies, consisting of isls. of St Kitts (St Christopher) and Nevis.

Area: 306 sq km (118 sq mi).

Population: 46,300 (est. 1984).

Capital: Basseterre (on St Kitts).

Language: English.

Religion: Christian.

Forested; economy based on sugar cane; some tourism. British colony with Anguilla from 1783; became associate state 1967; independent 1983; British Commonwealth member.

**Flag**: adopted in 1983; the colours represent fertility (green), sunshine (yellow), the independence struggle (red), the African heritage (black); the stars stand for hope and liberty.


**St LUCIA,** isl. of SE West Indies.

Area: 616 sq km (238 sq mi).

Population: 124,000 (est. 1982).

Capital: Castries.

Language: English.

Religion: Christian.

Scenic mts. with forested slopes; fruit, coconut exports. First settled in 17th cent.; possession changed hands between France and Britain until confirmed as British colony in 1814; associate state 1967; independent 1979; British Commonwealth member.

**Flag**: adopted in 1967; the symbol is said to represent the island's volcanic peaks rising from the sea.

**St VINCENT and the GRENADINES,** state of SE West Indies.
Area: 388 sq km (150 sq mi).
Population: 127,883 (est. 1982).
Capital: Kingstown.
Language: English.
Religion: Christian.
Well forested, mountainous; grows cotton; arrowroot, banana exports.
Settled by French, British, Dutch from 17th cent.; British colony from 1763; associate state 1969; independent 1979; British Commonwealth member.
**Flag**: adopted in 1979; the vertical tricolour displays the island's coat of arms on a breadfruit leaf on the central stripe.

**SAMOA, AMERICAN,** isl. group of C Pacific, situated NE of Fiji Isls.
Area: 200 sq km (77 sq mi).
Population. 32,297 (1980).
Capital: Pago Pago.
Languages: English, Samoan.
Religion: Christian.
Fruit growing, tuna fishing.
Discovered by Dutch 1722; divided between US and Germany 1899; self-government as overseas territ. of US 1960.
**Flag**: adopted in 1960; the bald eagle (representing the US) clutches the traditional Samoan symbols of authority, a chief's staff and knife.

**SAMOA, WESTERN,** isl. group of C Pacific, situated NE of Fiji Isls.

Area: 2850 sq km (1100 sq mi).

Population: 158,130 (1981).

Capital: Apia.

Languages: English, Samoan.

Religion: Christian.

Produces fruit, copra, cocoa.

Taken from Germany by New Zealand after WWII, held by them as UN trust territ.; independent 1962; British Commonwealth member.

**Flag:** adopted in 1948, amended in 1949; the red and white are the colours of the precolonial flags of the Samoan kingdom, and the stars represent the Southern Cross constellation.

**SAN MARINO,** republic of S Europe, enclave within E Italy.

Area: 62 sq km (24 sq mi).

Population: 22,053 (1983).

Capital: San Marino.

Language: Italian.

Religion: Roman Catholic.

Silk mfg.; agric. (exports wine, cattle); quarrying; tourism.

World's smallest republic, traditionally founded 4th cent.; placed itself under Italian protection 1862.

**Flag:** the colours derive from the state arms; the white is for the snowy mountains, the blue for the sky.

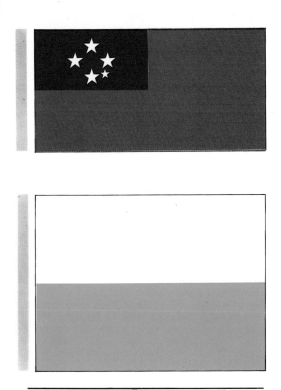

**SÃO TOMÉ and PRINCIPE,** W African republic, comprising 2 isls. in Gulf of Guinea.

Area: 964 sq km (372 sq mi).

Population: 113,000 (est. 1980).

Capital: São Tomé.

Language: Portuguese.

Religion: Roman Catholic.

Exports coffee, cacao, coconut products.

Discovered 1471; prov. of Portugal from 1522; independent 1975.

**Flag:** adopted in 1975, the Pan-African colours were used previously in this pattern by the liberation movement; the five-pointed stars represent the two islands.

**SAUDI ARABIA,** kingdom of SW Asia.

Area: *c* 2,149,690 sq km (830,000 sq mi).

Population: 9,160,000 (est. 1976).

Capital: Riyadh.

Language: Arabic.

Religion: Sunnite Islam.

Mainly desert; agric., pastoral economy; great wealth from rich oil deposits in E.

Has Islamic holy cities of Mecca, Medina; state formed 1932 following unification of Nejd and Hejaz in 1925.

**Flag:** adopted in 1938; the inscription above the sword reads 'There is no god but Allah, and Muhammad is the prophet of Allah'; the inscription is sewn separately on each side.

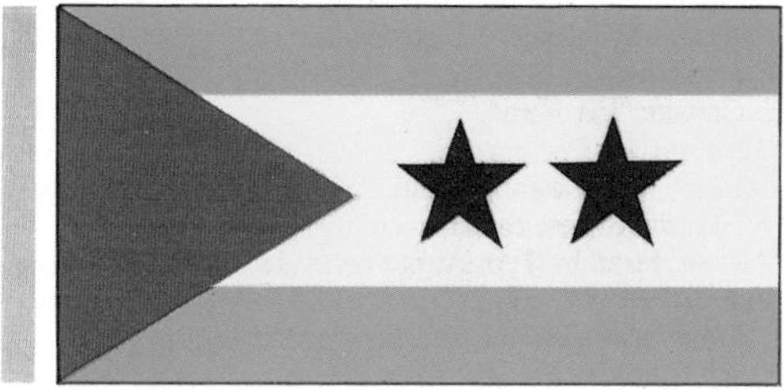

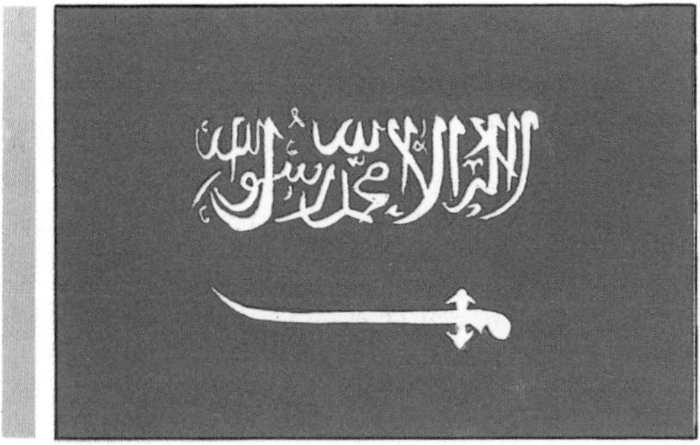
لا إله إلا الله محمد رسول الله

**SENEGAL,** republic of W Africa.
Area: 196,000 sq km (76,000 sq mi).
Population: 5,661,000 (est. 1980).
Capital: Dakar.
Language: French.
Religion: Islam.
Mainly low-lying savannah; stock rearing; exports groundnuts, phosphates.
Part of French West Africa from 1895; part of Mali Federation 1959-60; independent 1960; formed Senegambia Confederation with Gambia 1982.
**Flag:** adopted in 1960; uses the Pan-African colours arranged in the form of a French tricolour; distinguished from that of Mali by an Islamic star in the central band.

**SEYCHELLES,** isl. group in W Indian Ocean, NE of Madagascar.
Area: *c* 380 sq km (150 sq mi).
Population: 64,410 (1983).
Capital: Victoria.
Language: English, French, Creole.
Religion: Christian.
Volcanic isls.; coconuts, fish, copra, cinnamon, guano exports.
Known from 16th cent.; French territ. from 18th cent., ceded to British 1814; independent 1976; British Commonwealth member.
**Flag:** design adopted in 1977 from the flag of the dominant political party; the wavy pattern is said to represent the Indian Ocean.

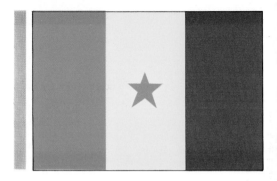

**SIERRA LEONE,** republic of W Africa.
Area: 71,700 sq km (27,700 sq mi).
Population: 3,470,000 (est. 1980).
Capital: Freetown.
Language: English.
Religions: native, Christian, Islam.
Coastal swamps, rising inland to wooded plateau; grows rice; exports diamonds, iron ore, bauxite.
Slave trade 17th-18th cent.; Freetown area became British colony 1808; hinterland incl. in protect. 1896; independent 1961; British Commonwealth member.
**Flag**: adopted in 1961, the colours derive from the coat of arms; green represents agriculture, white for peace, and blue for the Atlantic Ocean.


**SINGAPORE,** isl. republic off Malay penin.
Area: 583 sq km (225 sq mi).
Population: 2,502,400 (est. 1983).
Capital: Singapore.
Languages: Malay, Mandarin, Tamil, English.
Religions: Buddhism, Hinduism, Islam.
One of the largest seaports in the world; mfg. industries; international trade.
British colony 1824-1963; joined Malaysia on independence 1963, seceded 1965; population largely Chinese; British Commonwealth member.
**Flag**: adopted in 1959; red represents universal brotherhood, white purity; the crescent represents the nation's ascent, guided by the five stars of democracy, peace, progress, justice and equality.

**SOLOMON ISLANDS,** state of SW Pacific, E of New Guinea.

Area: *c* 29,800 sq km (11,500 sq mi).

Population: 244,000 (est. 1982).

Capital: Honiara.

Languages: Solomon Islands Pidgin, English.

Religion: Christian.

Exports timber, fish, copra, palm oil.

Discovered 1567; Britain estab. Solomon Isls. protect. 1889; independent 1977; British Commonwealth member.

**Flag**: adopted in 1978; the five stars represent the five districts, while the green is said to represent the land, the yellow the sun, and blue the sea (or the rivers).


**SOMALIA,** republic of E Africa.

Area: 637,000 sq km (246,200 sq mi).

Population: 5,000,000 (est. 1983).

Capital: Mogadishu.

Language: Somali.

Religion: Islam.

Coastal lowland, arid interior plateau; nomadic pastoralism; exports bananas, livestock, hides.

Formed 1960 from union of British and Italian Somaliland (latter a UN trust territ. from 1950); territorial clashes with Ethiopia.

**Flag**: adopted in 1954; the colours are those of the UN, and the five points of the star are said to stand for the five Somali areas.

**SOUTH AFRICA,** republic of S Africa.
Area: 1,221,000 sq km (471,500 sq mi).
Population: 29,290,000 (est. 1980).
Capitals: Cape Town (legislative), Pretoria (administrative), Bloemfontein (judicial).
Languages: Afrikaans, English.
Religion: Christian.
Mainly plateau, fringed by mts; grows cereals, fruit, sugar cane, vines; great mineral wealth.
Dutch settlement estab. 1652; annexed by UK 1806; British victory in Boer War 1899-1902; republic from 1960; withdrew from Commonwealth 1961.
**Flag:** dates from 1928, retained in 1961; the central stripe displays the Union Jack and the flags of the Orange Free State and the Transvaal.

**SPAIN,** kingdom of SW Europe.
Area: 505,000 sq km (195,000 sq mi).
Population: 37,682,355 (1981).
Capital: Madrid.
Language: Spanish.
Religion: Roman Catholic.
Pyrenees in NE, C plateau between Cantabrian Mts. (N), Sierra Morena (S); agric. incl. fruit, olives, wine, livestock; minerals; tourism.
Christian reconquest from Moors completed 1492; empire *fl* under Hapsburgs; republic 1931; Fascist victory in Civil War 1936-39; democracy from 1977.
**Flag:** the Nationalist design was adopted in 1938; the colours date back to the old kingdom of Aragon in the 12th cent.

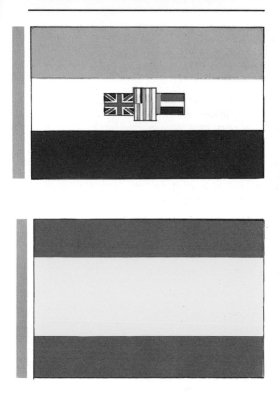

**SRI LANKA,** republic off SE coast of India.

Area: 65,600 sq km (25,300 sq mi).

Population: 14,800,001 (1981).

Capital: Colombo.

Language: Sinhalese.

Religion: Buddhism.

Central mts. with broad coastal plain; grows rice, rubber, coconuts, tea.

Dutch control from 17th to late 18th cent.; annexed by British 1815; independent as Ceylon 1948; republic 1956; native name adopted 1972.

**Flag**: adopted in 1948, amended 1951, 1972; the lion banner represents the ancient Buddhist kingdom, the two stripes the minority groups, green for the Muslims, orange for the Tamils.


**SUDAN,** republic of NE Africa.

Area: 2,505,800 sq km (967,500 sq mi).

Population: 19,500,000 (est. 1984).

Capital: Khartoum.

Language: Arabic.

Religions: Islam, native.

Nubian desert in NE, savannah in C, forest, swamps in S; grows millet; livestock; exports cotton.

Unified by Egyptians 1883-5; taken by Kitchener 1898; ruled as Anglo-Egyptian condominium until independence 1956.

**Flag**: adopted in 1969; uses the Pan-Arab colours to represent the independence struggle (red), Islam and peace (white), the nation (black), with a green triangle for prosperity and agriculture.

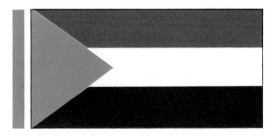

**SURINAM,** republic of NE South America.
Area: 63,037 sq km (163,266 sq mi).
Population: 390,000 (est. 1980).
Capital: Paramaribo.
Languages: Dutch, English.
Religion: Christian.
Coastal lowlands rise to forested highlands in S; coffee, rum, timber, bauxite exports.
Region disputed by English, Dutch; resolved 1815; named Dutch Guiana; renamed 1948; ceased being colony 1954, fully independent 1975.
**Flag**: design based on that of the main political parties, adopted in 1975; the yellow star represents unity and the nation's golden future.


**SWAZILAND,** kingdom of SE Africa.
Area: 17,350 sq km (6,700 sq mi).
Population: 600,000 (est. 1984).
Capital: Mbabane.
Languages: Swati, English.
Religions: Christian, native.
Veld areas from W to E; crops incl. maize, fruit, sugar, cotton; cattle rearing; coal, iron mining.
Independent from Zulus in 19th cent.; British protect. from 1906; independent 1968; British Commonwealth member.
**Flag**: adopted in 1968, based on that of the Swazi Pioneer Corps of WWII; the emblem dates back to 1890, and displays the weapons of a warrior – an oxhide shield, two assegai, and a fighting stick.

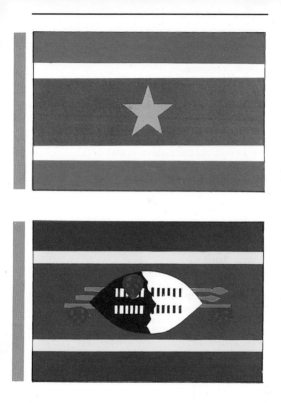

**SWEDEN,** kingdom of N Europe.
Area: 449,748 sq km (173,648 sq mi).
Population: 8,327,484 (1982).
Capital: Stockholm.
Language: Swedish.
Religion: Lutheranism.
Mts. in N, W, lakes in S; agric. mainly wheat, dairying; timber; iron ore; h.e.p.
United with Norway, Denmark in 1397; independent kingdom from 1523; united with Norway 1814-1905; has maintained neutral status in 20th cent.
**Flag**: adopted in 1906, dates back to mid-16th cent.; the colours derive from the national coat of arms of three gold crowns on blue, which dates back to 1364.

**SWITZERLAND,** federal republic of WC Europe.
Area: 41,285 sq km (15,940 sq mi).
Population: 6,365,960 (est. 1982).
Capital: Berne.
Languages: German, French, Italian.
Religions: Protestant, Roman Catholic.
Plateau in C, Alps in S, E; produces cheese, milk, confectionery, watches; banking; tourism.
Confederation estab. 1291 for defence against Hapsburgs; independent 1648; French occupation 1798-1815; Treaty of Paris estab. neutrality 1815.
**Flag**: adopted in 1848; a white cross on a red shield has been the Swiss emblem since the 14th cent.

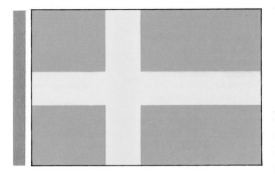

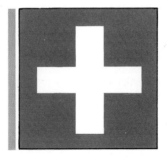

**SYRIA,** republic of SW Asia.
Area: 185,000 sq km (71,000 sq mi).
Population: 10,400,000 (est. 1981).
Capital: Damascus.
Language: Arabic.
Religion: Islam.
Bounded by Anti-Lebanon Mts. in W and Syrian desert in S; fertile valleys; exports cotton; oil.
Part of Ottoman Empire 1516-1918; mandated to France 1920; independent 1944; joined Egypt and Yemen in UAR 1958-61; dominated by Ba'ath Party.
**Flag**: the UAR flag (see Egypt) was adopted in 1972; the hawk emblem has been replaced by two green stars to represent Islam.


**TAIWAN,** isl. republic of E Asia.
Area: *c* 36,000 sq km (13,900 sq mi).
Population: 18,203,000 (1982).
Capital: Taipei.
Language: Mandarin Chinese.
Religion: Buddhism.
Crossed N-S by mts.; tropical climate; produces rice, timber, sugar; mining; fisheries.
Settled 17th cent. by Chinese after expulsion of Dutch; ceded to Japan 1895-1945; Nationalist govt. after 1949; withdrew from UN 1971.
**Flag**: the Kuomintang flag of Sun Yat-sen was adopted in 1949; the canton represents the blue heavens with a white sun, and the red field represents China.

**TANZANIA,** republic of E Africa.
Area: 945,000 sq km (364,000 sq mi).
Population: 17,551,925 (1978).
Capital: Dar-es-Salaam.
Languages: Swahili, English.
Religions: native, Islam, Christian.
Narrow coastal plain, interior plateau with volcanic peaks cut by Great Rift valley; exports coffee, cotton, sisal, diamonds.
Tanganyika part of German East Africa from 1884; British mandate 1916; independent 1961; united with Zanzibar 1964; British Commonwealth member.
**Flag**: adopted in 1964; the colours represent agriculture (green), mineral wealth (yellow), the people (black), water and Zanzibar (blue).


**THAILAND,** kingdom of SE Asia.
Area: *c* 514,000 sq km (198,500 sq mi).
Population: 49,459,000 est. 1983).
Capital: Bangkok.
Language: Thai.
Religion: Hinayana Buddhism.
Rice-producing C plain; mainly agric. economy; produces teak, tin, tungsten, rubber.
Siamese kingdom 14th cent.; frequent wars with Burma; lost territ. to British and French in 19th-20th cent.; constitutional monarchy 1932.
**Flag**: two red and white stripes are all that remains of the traditional red-on-white elephant emblem; the blue stripe was added in 1917 to show solidarity with the allies in WWI.

**TOGO,** republic of W Africa.
Area: 57,000 sq km (22,000 sq mi).
Population: 2,470,000 (est. 1979).
Capital: Lomé.
Official language: French.
Religions: animist, Roman Catholic.
Tropical forest in N, savannah in S; exports cacao, coffee, copra, phosphates.
Formerly French Togoland; formed 1922 from part of former German protect. under League of Nations mandate; independent 1960.
**Flag**: adopted in 1960; the Pan-African colours here represent agriculture (green), mineral wealth (yellow), bloodshed and struggle (red); the white star represents national purity.


**TONGA,** kingdom of S Pacific Ocean, E of Fiji Isls., S of Samoa.
Area: 675 sq km (260 sq mi).
Population: 98,000 (est. 1981).
Capital: Nuku'alofa.
Languages: Tongan, English.
Religion: Wesleyan Methodism.
Coral and volcanic isls.; exports copra, fruit.
Discovered by Dutch 1616; named Friendly Isles by Cook 1773; under British protection from 1900; independent 1970; British Commonwealth member.
**Flag**: adopted in 1875 on the understanding that it would never be altered, the flag represents the islanders' total commitment to Methodism.

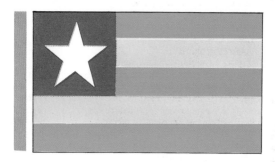

**TRINIDAD and TOBAGO,** republic of SE West Indies.
Area: 5129 sq km (1980 sq mi).
Population: 1,055,800 (est. 1980).
Capital: Port of Spain.
Language: English.
Religion: Protestant, Roman Catholic.
Hilly interior; tropical climate; grows sugar cane, fruits; asphalt, oil refining industs.
Discovered by Columbus 1498; ceded to Britain 1802; part of Federation of West Indies 1958-62; republic 1976; British Commonwealth member.
**Flag:** adopted in 1962; red represents the people's warmth and vitality, black their strength and the islands' wealth, white their hopes and the sea.


**TUNISIA,** republic of N Africa.
Area: 164,200 sq km (63,400 sq mi).
Population: 6,520,000 (est. 1981).
Capital: Tunis.
Languages: Arabic, French.
Religion: Islam.
Atlas Mts. in N, Sahara in S; produces wheat, dates, olives, grapes; exports phosphates, petroleum, iron ore; fishing; tourism.
*Fl* 13th-16th cent. under Berbers; fell to Turks, became Barbary pirate base; occupied by France 1881; independent 1956; republic 1957.
**Flag:** adopted in 1835, based on the flag of Turkey, retained in 1956; the star and crescent are traditional Islamic symbols.

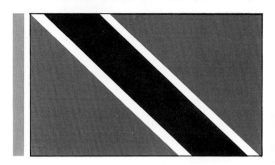

**TURKEY,** republic of Asia Minor and SE Europe.
Area: 781,000 sq km (296,000 sq mi).
Population: 45,217,556 (1980).
Capital: Ankara.
Language: Turkish.
Religion: Islam.
Mainly arid plateau crossed by mts. in N and S; produces wheat, barley, tobacco, fruit; minerals incl. coal, copper, chromium.
Invaded by Seljuk Turks in 11th cent., then centre of Ottoman Empire; declined after defeat at Vienna 1683; republic, major reforms under Ataturk 1923.
**Flag**: regularized in 19th cent., retained in 1923; the crescent is an ancient Turkish and Islamic symbol, the star was added in the early 19th cent.

**TURKS and CAICOS ISLANDS,** isls. SE of Bahamas, N of Hispaniola.
Area: 430 sq km (166 sq mi).
Population: 7,436 (1984).
Capital: Grand Turk.
Language: English.
Religion: Christian.
Salt, crayfish exports; expanding tourism.
Discovered 1512; settled in 17th cent.; admin. by Jamaica 1873-1962; British crown colony from 1962; internal self-government from 1976.
**Flag**: flies the Blue Ensign; the coat of arms contains a conch shell, a spiny lobster and a turk's head cactus.

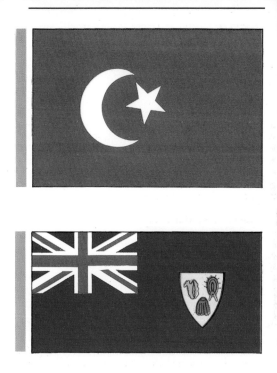

**TUVALU,** isl. group of SW Pacific Ocean, NE of Solomon Isls.

Area: 23 sq km (9 sq mi).

Population: 7,349 (est. 1979).

Capital: Funafuti.

Language: English.

Religion: Protestant.

Coral atolls; produces copra; philatelic sales.

Formerly (as Ellice Isls.) part of the Gilbert and Ellice Isls. colony; independent 1978; British Commonwealth member.

**Flag:** the Blue Ensign with a light blue field was adopted in 1978; the nine gold stars show the positions of the main islands.

**UGANDA,** republic of EC Africa.

Area: 236,000 sq km (91,100 sq mi)

Population: 12,600,000 (est. 1980).

Capital: Kampala.

Languages: Bantu, English.

Religions: native, Christian, Islam.

Mainly plateau, bordered by lakes and mts.; tropical savannah; grows cotton, coffee; forestry; industs. based on copper ores; h.e.p.

Buganda became British protect. 1894; territ. added 1896; independent 1962; coups in 1966, 1971, 1979, 1985; British Commonwealth member.

**Flag:** adopted in 1962; the colours represent the people (black), the sun (yellow), and brotherhood (red); the central emblem is a crested crane.

**UNION OF SOVIET SOCIALIST REPUBLICS,** federal
republic of E Europe and Asia.
Area: *c* 22,402,000 sq km (8,649,000 sq mi).
Population: 273,843,000 (1984)
Capital: Moscow.
Language: Russian, and many minority languages.
Religion: Russian Orthodox.
Comprises 35 republics; underwent enormous indust.
growth from 1920s; great mineral wealth.
Russia founded by Rurik at Novgorod 862; Romanov
dynasty estab. 1613; social unrest led to Revolution in
1917 and estab. of USSR under Lenin.
**Flag**: adopted in 1923; the hammer represents industry,
the sickle agriculture, the star the Communist Party, the
red field revolution.


**UNITED ARAB EMIRATES,** group of 7 sheikdoms, SE
Arabia.
Area: *c* 84,000 sq km (32,400 sq mi).
Population: 1,300,000 (est. 1984).
Capital: Abu Dhabi.
Language: Arabic.
Religion: Islam.
Pearls, dried fish; oil at Abu Dhabi.
British protect. 1892-1971; known as Trucial States
prior to independence; comprises Abu Dhabi, Dubai,
Sharjah, Ras al Khaimah, Fujeitah, Ajman, Umm al
Qaiwain; see also Bahrain and Qatar.
**Flag**: the Pan-Arab colours were adopted in 1971; the
flags of the seven emirates are all red and white, and date
from a treaty of 1820 with Britain.

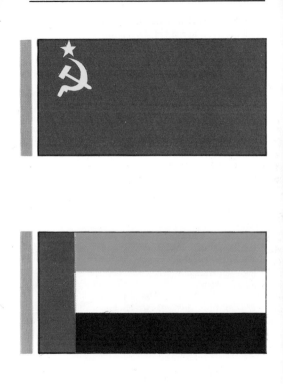

**UNITED KINGDOM,** island kingdom of NW Europe.
Area: 244,750 sq km (94,500 sq mi).
Population: 55,776,000 (1981).
Capital: London.
Language: English.
Religions: Protestant, Roman Catholic.
Incl. England, Scotland, Wales, Northern Ireland,
Channel Isls., Isle of Man.
Constitutional monarchy; called United Kingdom of
Great Britain and Northern Ireland after Irish partition
1921.
**Flag**: combines English, Scottish and Irish emblems;
dates from 1603, when James VI of Scotland became
James I of England; the Irish emblem was added on
union with Ireland in 1801.

**England**: St George's Cross

**Northern Ireland**: the six points of the star represent the six counties

**Scotland**: St Andrew's Cross

**Wales**: the red dragon of Cadwallader, Prince of Gwynned

**UNITED STATES,** federal republic of N America.
Area: 9,363,353 sq km (3,615,191 sq mi).
Population: 231,106,727 (1980).
Capital: Washington.
Language: English.
Religions: Protestant, Roman Catholic.
Grain-producing C plains; oilrich S; world's major industrial power.
Republic estab. after 1776 Revolution; Civil War 1861-5; dominant world power since WWII.
**Flag:** the 1775 Revolutionary flag had 9 red and white stripes representing the revolting colonies; Union Jack in the canton replaced with stars 1777; from 1818 has borne 13 stripes for the 13 original colonies, a star being added for each new state.

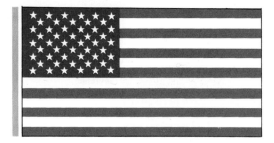

**1795 Flag**

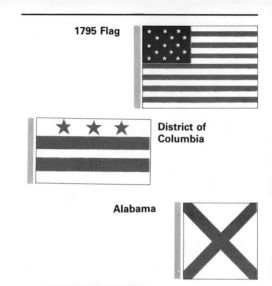

**District of Columbia**

**Alabama**

**Alaska**

**Arizona**

**Arkansas**

**California**

**Colorado**

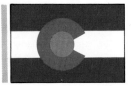

**Connecticut**

**Delaware**

**Florida**

**Georgia**

**Hawaii**

**Idaho**

**Illinois**

**Indiana**

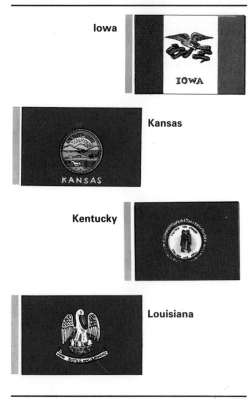

**Iowa**

**Kansas**

**Kentucky**

**Louisiana**

 **Maine**

**Maryland**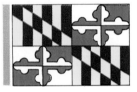

 **Massachusetts**

**Michigan**

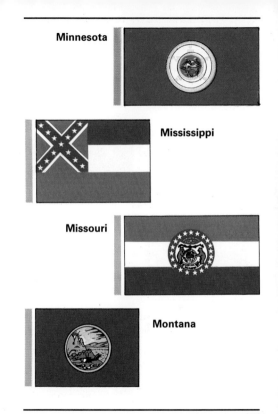

**Minnesota**

**Mississippi**

**Missouri**

**Montana**

**Nebraska**

**Nevada**

**New Hampshire**

**New Jersey**

**New Mexico**

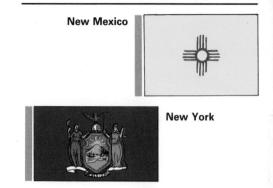

**New York**

**North Carolina**

**North Dakota**

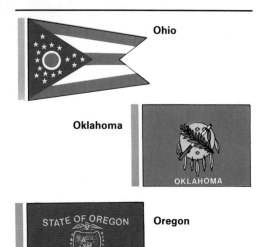

**Ohio**

**Oklahoma**

**Oregon**

**Pennsylvania**

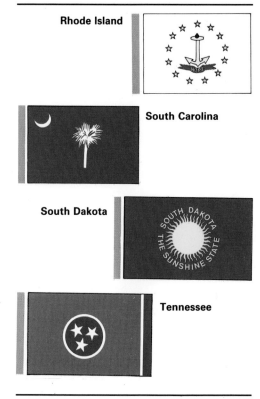

**Rhode Island**

**South Carolina**

**South Dakota**

**Tennessee**

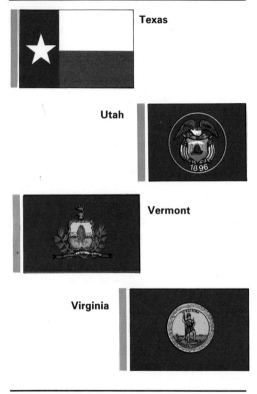

**Texas**

**Utah**

**Vermont**

**Virginia**

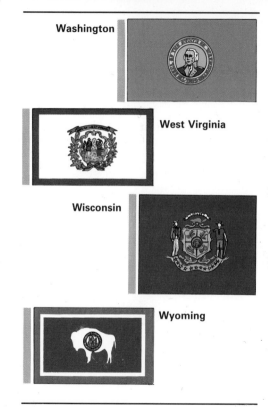

**Washington**

**West Virginia**

**Wisconsin**

**Wyoming**

**URUGUAY,** republic of SE South America.
Area: 177,508 sq km (68,536 sq mi).
Population: 2,886,187 (est. 1984).
Capital: Montevideo.
Language: Spanish.
Religion: Roman Catholic.
Fertile plains (wheat growing) rise to N grasslands
(sheep, cattle rearing).
Spanish-Portuguese struggle for possession 16th-17th
cent.; liberation from Spain 1810; claimed by Argentina
and Brazil; independent 1828.
**Flag**: adopted in 1830, the nine stripes represent the
original provinces; the blue and white colours and gold
sun derive from the flag of Argentina.


**VANUATU,** archipelago of SW Pacific Ocean, between
Australia and Fiji Isls.
Area: c 14,760 sq km (5,700 sq mi).
Population: 112,596 (1979).
Capital: Vila.
Languages: Bislama (Pidgin), English, French.
Religion: Christian.
Tropical climate; active volcanoes; produces copra,
manganese ore, tuna; tourism.
Formerly known as New Hebrides; UK-French con-
dominium estab. 1906; independent 1980; British
Commonwealth member.
**Flag**: adopted in 1980; displays a boar's horn in the
triangle in the hoist.

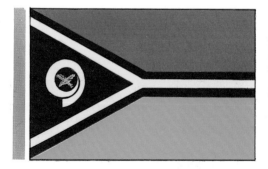

**VATICAN CITY,** independent papal state within Rome.
Area: 44 ha. (109 acres).
Population: 731 (1978).
Languages: Italian, Latin.
Religion: Roman Catholic.
Papacy lost much territ. in 19th cent. to Italian states;
new state created 1929 by Lateran Treaty; seat of govt.
of Roman Catholic church; incl. St Peter's Basilica;
libraries, museums contain priceless collections.
**Flag**: formerly the civil ensign of the Papal States,
adopted again in 1929; bears the triple tiara of the Popes
above the keys of Heaven given to St Peter.


**VENEZUELA,** republic of N South America.
Area: 912,050 sq km (352,143 sq mi).
Population: 14,516,735 (1981).
Capital: Caracas.
Language: Spanish.
Religion: Roman Catholic.
Coast (oil production) rises to E Andes (coffee, cacao);
cattle raising; gold, diamond mining.
Independence struggle under Simon Bolivar against
Spain 1811-21; part of Greater Columbia until 1830.
**Flag**: the colours were first used in 1806 (see Colombia
and Ecuador); the seven stars represent the seven
original provinces, and the state flag bears a coat of arms
in the canton.

**VIETNAM,** republic of SE Asia.
Area: *c* 333,000 sq km (128,000 sq mi).
Population: 60,000,000 (est. 1984).
Capital: Hanoi.
Language: Vietnamese.
Religion: Taoism.
Forested mts. and plateau with Mekong Delta in S; chief crop rice.
Formerly part of French Indochina; divided into North and South Vietnam after Geneva Convention 1954; war and US intervention from 1960s; unified following Northern (Communist) victory 1975.
**Flag:** used by Ho Chi Minh in the liberation struggle against Japan in WWII, adopted as the national flag by the Communists in 1945.

**VIRGIN ISLANDS, BRITISH,** isl. group in West Indies.
Area: 153 sq km (133 sq mi).
Population: 12,034 (1980).
Capital: Road Town.
Language: English.
Religion: Christian.
Mainly hilly islands; industry based on tourism, also cattle raising, fishing, vegetables, rum.
Discovered and named (1493) by Columbus; British colony from 17th cent.
**Flag:** the Blue Ensign displays the islands' badge, a virgin with 12 oil lamps from the parable in the Bible story (Matthew 25:1-13).

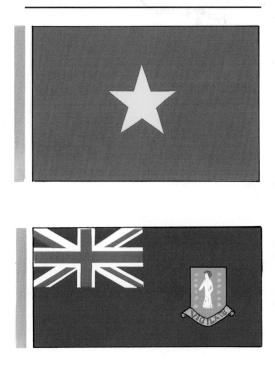

**VIRGIN ISLANDS OF THE UNITED STATES,** isl. group of West Indies, E of Puerto Rico.

Area: 345 sq km (133 sq mi).

Population: 96,569 (1980).

Capital: Charlotte Amalie.

Language: English.

Religion: Christian.

Isls. incl. St Thomas, St Croix, St John; warm climate; tourism; rum, textiles.

Purchased from Denmark 1917; inhabitants are US citizens.

**Flag:** adopted in 1921; based on the US coat of arms; displays the American bald eagle with a shield between the letters 'V' and 'I'.


**YEMEN ARAB REPUBLIC (North Yemen),** state of SW Asia, in Arabian penin.

Area: *c* 195,000 sq km (75,300 sq mi).

Population: 8,556,974 (est. 1984).

Capital: Sana.

Language: Arabic.

Religion: Sunnite Islam.

Coastal strip in W, mts., desert in interior; grows grains, fruit, coffee.

The Arabia Felix of the ancient world; under Turkish rule 1849-1918; member of UAR 1958-61; republic 1962.

**Flag:** adopted in 1962; based on the UAR flag (see Egypt); uses the Pan-Arab colours with a green Islamic star to represent Arab unity.

**YEMEN, PEOPLE'S DEMOCRATIC REPUBLIC OF (South Yemen),** state of SW Asia, in Arabian penin.
Area: *c* 287,500 sq km (111,000 sq mi).
Population: 1,800,000 (est. 1977).
Capital: Aden.
Language: Arabic.
Religion: Islam.
Coastal strip in S; mts. and plateau in interior; some indust., agric. and fishery development.
Ruled by UK from 1830s; Federation of South Arabia estab. 1963; republic 1967.
**Flag**: the National Liberation Front's flag using the Pan-Arab colours of the UAR flag (see Egypt) was adopted in 1967, with a pale blue triangle and red star (for revolution) added.

**YUGOSLAVIA,** federal republic of SE Europe.
Area: *c* 255,750 sq km (98,750 sq mi).
Population: 22,420,000 (est. 1981).
Capital: Belgrade.
Language: Mainly Serbo-Croat.
Religions: Orthodox, Roman Catholic, Islam.
Mts. run NW-SE; fertile lowlands in NE; cereals, forestry, livestock; coal, iron, copper; tourism.
Kingdom of Serbs, Croats, Slovenes created 1918, renamed Yugoslavia 1929; Communist republic under Tito estab. 1945 after partisan war against Nazis.
**Flag**: the Serbian (originally Russian) colours adopted in 1918 date from the early 19th cent. and represent Pan-Slav unity; in 1946 the coat of arms was replaced by the Communist star.

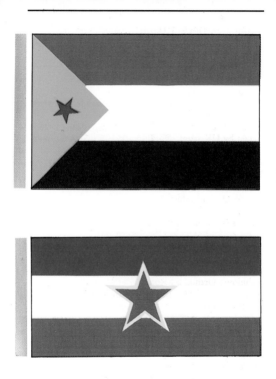

**ZAÏRE,** republic of C Africa.
Area: 905,400 sq km (345,000 sq mi).
Population: 28,400,000 (est. 1981).
Capital: Kinshasa.
Languages: Bantu, French.
Religions: native, Christian.
R. Zaïre basin; rain forest in N, savannah in S; produces cotton, coffee, timber, copper, diamonds.
Congo Free State estab. 1885; Belgian Congo colony 1908; independent republic 1960; Katanga secession and civil war 1960-5; renamed Zaïre 1971.
**Flag**: the Pan-African colours were adopted in 1971; the emblem is that of the Popular Movement, the torch representing the spirit of revolution and the lives of dead revolutionaries.

**ZAMBIA,** republic of SC Africa.
Area: 753,000 sq km (290,500 sq mi).
Population: 6,050,000 (est. 1982).
Capital: Lusaka.
Languages: Bantu, English.
Religions: native, Christian.
Mainly plateau, mts. in N, NE; savannah; agric. incl. maize, tobacco, coffee, livestock; copper.
British rule estab. by 1900; Northern Rhodesia protect. created 1924; independent 1964; British Commonwealth member.
**Flag**: the colours of the dominant political party were adopted in 1964; the eagle is said to represent freedom, the orange the nation's copper mines.

**ZIMBABWE,** republic of SC Africa.
Area: 391,000 sq km (151,000 sq mi).
Population: 7,539,000 (est. 1982).
Capital: Harare.
Languages: Bantu, English.
Religions: native, Christian.
Largely river-drained plateau; grows tobacco, stock raising; gold, asbestos, chrome, coal.
British rule estab. in 1890s; colony of Southern Rhodesia from 1924; declared UDI 1965; independent 1980; British Commonwealth member.
**Flag:** the colours of the liberation movement (see Mozambique for their meaning) were adopted in 1980; the star represents the nation's ideals, the soapstone bird is the national emblem.

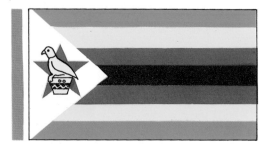